Pancakes Taste Like Poverty:
And Other Post-Divorce Revelations

© 2014 Lulu Author. All rights reserved.
ISBN 978-1-329-00442-9

For Shirley, Sherrie, Christopher
and
my babies most of all.

Preface

A box of condoms started all of this.
Well, to be perfectly honest it was a garbage can full of maggots, as you'll soon learn, and then a box of condoms.
You see, I was ten years into an obligatory marriage when, during a family trip to get blueberry pancakes, I opened the glove box of my then-husband's car to stow away my cumbersome clutch and came to find a bright blue box of condoms tucked away inside.
He froze. His face was all guilt, remorse, fear, panic, mouth agape, eyes wide. But I was awash with calm and blessed with a surprising lightness and relief.
There was only one option. This was the end. This box of condoms was just one in a long list of symptoms of a poisonous, destructive marriage.
I was staring right at my exit, my reality, my last straw.
The last straw wasn't the time he skipped our first Christmas together to do cocaine all night.
The last straw wasn't the time he cheated with the checkout girl from the title loan shop.
The last straw wasn't the fact that the kids and I went without dental or medical care while he collected RC cars and swords and went on yoga retreats.
The last straw wasn't when we moved into his parents house, having lost our house, and him asking if he could date one of his former classmates.
And the last straw wasn't the love letter I found written to one of his ex-girlfriends a few weeks earlier.

Nope, *this* was it.

Shortly thereafter I scraped together enough money for a deposit on an apartment nearby. We'd been saving to get a house and move out of his parents house. I called my mom to help with the rest. Our belongings had been absorbed into his family with his siblings and parents borrowing and using and rarely replacing or returning. Boxes of our memories had been shoved into the deepest corners of closets and garages.
I didn't care.
I just wanted out.
So I took my three children, a few backpacks of clothing and a mattress that his mother offered me and left the rest behind. The mattress was twenty years old, bowed in the middle, chewed by dogs and peed on by my bed-wetting children.
It was more than enough. I just wanted out.
And so there I was with three kids looking to me to handle everything. The fear couldn't show. The pain couldn't show. I had to be strong for them. And so, I took to journaling or, rather, blogging as a means of relieving the pressure.
I just needed to be heard.
What follows are my blog posts between 2011 and 2014. During that period I contemplated prostitution, dreamed about suicide, ate a lot of beans, moved, met amazing people, rebuilt myself, learned some parenting lessons, got Catfished, went back to college twice and found love.
In addition to my blog posts are entries from a personal diary I was keeping at the time with the

intention of publishing on the blog which never made it for one reason or another.

Reading my blog posts now, the ups and downs seem to happen very quickly and I go from feeling powerful and full of light to murderous and sorrowful within a few sentences. I apologize in advance. But, if anything, it's an honest account of the post-divorce rollercoaster.

I'd like to thank my mother for supporting me so endlessly, my sister for being my champion, my father and stepmother for depositing parcels of wisdom into my heart, the crazy blonde lady for showing me what community and solidarity mean, all my sisterwolves who roam and hunt together, my children who are so wise and patient, and Christopher, one of the loves of my life.

And thank you, dear reader.

J. Viv

TAMPA

Stuffed – February 2011

I'm Jessica.
I'm twenty-nine.
I'm a mom of three.
I'm very recently single after almost a decade of marriage.
Yes, that would mean I got married before I could drink legally.
No, I don't know what the hell I was thinking.

Getting divorced feels a bit like leaving one of those cults Dr. Phil is always trying to infiltrate. Any hopeful moments of freedom-triggered ecstasy is met with the terrifying and nauseating realization that you don't know anything and the rest of the world evolved and expanded while you wiped spit-up from your bargain bin maternity tee.

I spent my entire adult life identifying myself with the moods, thoughts and idiosyncrasies of one person.

Add to that a lonely, latch-key childhood and an almost insatiable addiction to male attention and you're left with one seriously lost individual.

And so my quest begins to…

(I can hardly type it, clichés make me gag)

…to…find myself.

Really. I don't know how else to say it.

Or, instead of finding myself, I am building myself. I'm sewing all the pieces together, stuffing myself with the love and attention I wasted on others, picking out a cute little outfit to wear so that I am irresistible to shoppers.

There are some things I *do* know:

I know I'm funny.
I know I'm a good friend.
I like to cook.
I want Joseph Gordon-Levitt to be my next ex-husband.
I love the Earth.
My belief system is not exactly mainstream.
I'm a good mom.
I was a good wife.

The rest will fall into place.

I think that was another cliché. Sorry. I'll work on that.

The Beginning of the End

What's interesting about leaving a marriage is that what looks like the end is never the end for the person who's choosing to go.

My eventual acceptance of my dead marriage came in the form of a few pivotal moments. It wasn't the fights or the drama or the transgressions. There were so many I couldn't begin to remember them all. But I do remember when the Universe first whispered for me to go.

It was 2009 and we had been fighting for days. I have no idea what about. I was taking out the trash. I could hear the garbage truck coming.

I lifted the lid of the giant trash can, already teeming with this week's batch of maggots, and the top-heavy container tipped over, spilling rotten food, fermenting garbage water and maggots all over my driveway.

And then it hit me.

Right in the chest.

A sledgehammer.
But the pain never let up.
I gasped.

I couldn't get air.

A fist was squeezing my heart.

Tighter and tighter

I collapsed on the driveway.

No air.

Blackness.

Stars.

Slow down.

Breathe.

With each desperate gasp I could feel my throat closing, despite my attempts to control my body. My heart was pounding in my ears.

I don't want my kids to find me. I don't want to die in my driveway.

I don't want to die.

I don't want to die fat.

I don't want to die uneducated.

I don't want the last decade to be the way I spent my adult life.

I don't want this to be the last day.

I heard a voice through the muddy drumming of my heartbeat. A vague figure came toward me. There was the faint, fruity stench of the garbage truck.

You are in control.

The drumming slowed.

You are in control.

I forced my lungs to work *for* me.

This marriage will kill you.

The garbage man helped me up and insisted we call an ambulance. Having no insurance, I insisted he didn't.

I think it was a panic attack. It could have been a heart attack. Either way, the message was clear. My marriage was going to kill me. Maybe not immediately, but the stress and the holding in and the lack of respect/love/excitement/trust – all of it – would kill me.

I looked at my life as someone's wife: I didn't finish college. I quit a job I was good at and that I loved, to support my husband's goals. I was forty pounds overweight. I was sleepy. I was angry. I was vengeful. I was getting migraines. I was miserable.

And one day, I will die.

There is nothing – absolutely not ONE thing – more valuable or precious than peace of mind. It's not security It's not what-your-family-will-think. It's not the-next-obvious-step-in-the-relationship.

Nothing.

From that point on, I told myself that even if I file for divorce and then turn around and get struck by a truck the fact that I *finally* put my happiness on the to-do list would be worth it. It would be worth it for my two girls. It would be worth it for my son.

I do not believe, for a second, that I will get a gold star when I die and go to Heaven or wherever on my how-I-lived-my-life essay for my "Excellent Martyrdom."

I had become one of those Oprah makeover "before" moms, something I had vowed NEVER to be. When I was just me, I thought I'd be a cast member on SNL or an English teacher or a sex therapist.

I was none of the above.

I was not much aside from embarrassed and ashamed.

How did I get there?

How did I get to the driveway, in Mobile, Alabama, covered in garbage juice, with a maggot in my hair, having a panic attack, with three barefoot kids in my rented house.

HOW!?!?!

And more importantly, how the hell do I get out?

That was the day. That was when the seed was planted.
I did not immediately file for divorce but we talked about it.
Shortly after that, we found out we were getting evicted and decided to give each other "one last try" by starting afresh in Tampa, Florida near his family.
Shortly after that the five of us were living in two rooms in his parents house, forced witnesses to their own crumbling marriage.
Shortly after that he dated other women and wrote love notes to even more.
And shortly after that, I saved myself and left.

Moving Day

He and I had a tendency to overestimate our ability to earn a living. We were perpetual minimalists; chronic purgers.

If we didn't want to move something, we just threw it away.

This wasn't my natural state, but he conditioned me to be this way.

Only now, looking back, I know this is a manipulation tactic.

When we first moved in together after finding out I was pregnant with our first child, while packing the things from my single-girl apartment he edited me aggressively.

My beloved New Kids on the Block blanket that I'd had since I was ten, soft and heavily hugged. It was THE most comfortable thing. I used it to envelop drunk friends who stayed the night and they always woke up expressing exactly that.

"This blanket is THE most comfortable thing."

It had to go because it was "stupid."

I went to the same small private school from first grade until graduation. Like all kids, the majority of my formative years were spent at school. It was my dysfunctional family. My yearbooks were my dysfunctional family album.

They had to go because they were "heavy."

Piece by piece my "before" was erased and being so young and so scared and so desperate I didn't put up much of a fight.

The pictures of his pre-Jessica partying and pre-Jessica girlfriends became shrined in his memories and got to stay despite my protests.

It was so subtle but so obvious looking back.

But then I didn't know anything. I was brainless.

So again, when I was manipulated into leaving my turf and coming back to Tampa, I was advised to leave it all behind because "the kids and I are already here, just bring what you can fit in your car. We can replace the stuff. It's just stuff."

This resulted in ten years of existence being reduced to little more than a few boxes of essential books and photo albums, suitcases of clothing and little else.

We were "starting over."

This proved to be extremely inconvenient when it was time to move out on my own.

When we moved into his parents' house it was made clear our presence, rightfully, was not exactly welcome.

It wasn't long before our boxes got shoved and dumped and upended into random closets already stuffed to the brim with however many years worth of his parents' stuff.

The archaeological mission of finding our things, which had already been squished and integrated into *their* things was, frankly, not worth it.

I just wanted out.

I wanted *out*.

I did manage to find one box of books.
I never found another, full of my smutty books of erotica and studies of Japanese sex clubs. It is still lost, somewhere, in my conservative Christian ex-mother-in-law's house both to my dismay and delight.
My in-laws let me take the mattress our family had been sleeping on. My kids had taken to bed-wetting and the twenty-something year old mattress had already been chewed by its previous occupant's pet Chihuahuas.
It was holey and pissy and, apparently, now mine.
And that was about it.
I'd been planning my escape for longer than I realized, squirreling away money when I worked at my last job as a hotel concierge. I'd been away from that job for about six months under his advice. The schedule was too hard with three little ones and getting them to school was too much. I should just let him handle the work and bills and find another job with a better schedule.
With this squirreled money and a huge, huge amount from my mom I was able to get an apartment less than five minutes from the majority of his family. I had no family nor friends of my own in Tampa so I figured close would be better.
His mom and I moved my three boxes, three kids, piss-mattress and I to the new place.
And despite having no furniture, no toiletries, no groceries, no toys and now, no father in the home my kids were shockingly...light.
They were giggly and happy and buoyant and sunshiny.
To them, the lack didn't matter. This place was new and it was *ours*.
It was *ours*.

We didn't have to follow his mom's rules or dodge his dad. We didn't have that constant unwelcome guest feeling. We could do whatever we wanted.
I should have been relieved that my kids were adjusting so well but honestly, it stung. This could have been my kids all along. I'd kept them from feeling like this. Because *I* wanted to make it work with their father. I was so caught up in trying to make peace and do what's right that I didn't even notice the effect all of the dysfunction had on my kids. They were the way they were because life had always been the way it was. And life with him was unpredictable, mad, unstable, highly sensitive, fragile, precarious, dizzying, obligatory...
And my kids had developed coping strategies or no strategies at all. And I thought it was just "who they were." But it wasn't...
In "doing what's right" I'd actively taken place in the breaking of my children. And here I was, in my absolute darkest and most lacking and I was seeing them for the first time *ever*.

But they'd seen me. They'd seen him and his family and all of it.
I hadn't protected them from anything. I'd exposed them to far too much by doing "what's right."
But the apartment was the end of that and the beginning of putting us first.
For lunch that day we had pizza. We ate it on the floor near the piss-mattress in the living room and huddled watching DVDs on my laptop. Then we unpacked what little we had and giggled and checked in with the family.
His sisters came by gifting us our first set of much needed and much appreciated groceries.
As night fell, we realized we didn't have lamps for any of the rooms with the only light coming from the bathroom.
That's an easy fix. We can get lamps.
I was just so happy to cuddle and hold my new children. Their energy fed me.
But alas it was time for dinner so we decided to reheat the leftover pizza in the oven. But when I

went to retrieve the piping hot pizza to deliver it to my bright, delighted children who were high on the novelty of the new space I realized I had no oven mitts.

And I had no towels.
I had no rubber gloves.
I had no paper towels.
I had no tongs.
I had no forks.
I had no foil.
I had absolutely no method of retrieving the pizza from the oven.
It was at that moment I realized:

Jessica,

You're fucked.

D-Day

The process of the actual divorce was easy - too easy I would later find out. Since I had no money it was cheap to file. Since we had no things there was nothing to split.

I literally printed the divorce off the county clerk's website and filled it out myself. I decided on a reasonable amount for child support and mapped out visitation.

Neither was an issue.

He had since been kicked out of his parents' house and was living with a roommate somewhere across town. Since his living situation was less conducive to overnight stays he would come spend the weekends at the apartment with us.

It seems strange but I had no anger toward him. There was nothing to fight about. So we could get on co-parenting and just being teammates without all the messy business of loving each other or being faithful or sober.

He could spend his week being as drunk and promiscuous as he pleased. I didn't know. It wasn't my business anymore and I didn't care.

He came on Friday night with some cash for us and cooked dinner and snuggled the kids and threw them around like dads do and it worked.

In a bizarre and only-in-a-TV-movie way when our court date for the official divorce was assigned it was identical to that of his parents who had since split also.

When D-day arrived neither of us bothered to get very dressed. He wore jeans and flip flops. My wardrobe consisted of jeans and two or three shirts so I had no choice but to wear them.

We arrived early to be met a few minutes later by his parents – separately – each with a friend for moral support. With sad eyes they gave us "understanding" hugs and pats while we, in our flip-flops, giggled and chit-chatted.

Finally we were called in to the room with half a dozen other non-contested, quick-divorce couples. They were called up one by one to swear the marriage was irreparable, sign the papers and leave.

My husband, being named after his father and *his* father and *his* father, was called up with me.

We swore and signed – eagerly.

The judge, confused, called up his father with the same name.

"Wait a second," he halted us, "you're getting divorced today and your parents are getting divorced today?"

We nodded.

"You can't make that up. What a tragic day."

But it wasn't a tragic day for us. For me, it was one of the best days. It was maybe the first authentic thing I'd ever done. And *he* was free. Not of his responsibility but of the role of husband. He was not ready and he knew it. And I was tired. We'd tried for ten years. It didn't feel like a failure.

We waited outside the courtroom to say goodbye to his parents.

"What are you guys doing now?" His father asked.

"We're going to go eat pancakes at the IHOP where we met," my ex answered cheerfully.

And with that we high-fived (literally) and skipped (literally) down the hallway to our new uncertain future.

I wish I could say everything has been as smooth and amicable as the day we got divorced. But, for what it's worth, it was a shockingly pleasant day.

Spencer and Maya

Spencer and Maya are the two jackasses who live in the downstairs apartment.

Spencer is twenty-two. He is one of those guys who is simultaneously hot and repulsive. Like he's hot, no doubt. He looks like Josh Hartnett (hot) but if Hartnett had been raised in a really dodgy trailer park and had been in and out of prison on various drug charges (repulsive).

His uniform is a white tank top and baggy sweatpants with his boxers showing. He almost always has a cellphone in one hand, a cigarette in the other. He sits on the third from bottom step, talking loudly either to women or his friends to whom he complains about the aforementioned women being "jealous bitches who love drama."

While he does this, he spits his smoker-phlegm onto the bottom step leaving a slippery sheen of gray-yellow mucus for myself and Other Single Mom next door to hop over every time we go up and down the stairs because it is *that* slippery. When we're lucky, it rains and washes the phlegm away, leaving the bottom stair splatter-bleached by whatever strange chemical composition Spencer's phlegm possesses. The step now resembles a concrete version of acid wash.

Despite being gross, he is dangerously aware of how narrow and gray the gross/hot delineation is and he lives right in the middle of it.

After his louder fights with his live-in girlfriend, when I have my eyebrows fixed and I am ready to confront him, he leans in close and smoothly apologizes with the most charismatic husky whisper. And I remember that one day I might need his help moving furniture (or he could, like, punch me in the face) and I wave him off with a lackluster finger-wag and return to minding my business.

As for his girlfriend, Maya, she is nineteen. She looks like a black Snookie when Snookie was doing the hair bump and leopard print, only Maya's hair bump is made of that plastic-looking weave that looks like Barbie hair. She wears big hoop earrings and her vapid nature comes through when she speaks. You know, like she speaks in gravelly whisper-giggle with plenty of upspeak thrown in, just in case you thought there was promise for a decent conversation.

I know she works somewhere, so I assume she pays most of the bills. She tends to keep to herself until it's time for a throwdown.

Almost weekly, Maya confronts Spencer about the other girls he is talking to, or his drug use, or the abortion he talked her into which we know about because Spencer talks about it loudly on the phone at midnight to whomever. Almost weekly, Spencer reacts by getting loud. Maya throws things. She runs outside, threatening to get in the car and leave, but never does. She gets on the phone with people telling them to come get her for real this time, that she'll text them when she's packed, that there is no going back. Spencer gets on *his* phone and sits on the step smoking and complaining about how crazy she is, taking breaks to spit, take a drag from his ever-present cigarette or yell at her about how crazy she is.

I usually stay out of it because I want to be neither ally nor enemy to either of these kids.

Other Single Mom, however, is ten years older than me and clearly gives fewer fucks. She steps outside and threatens to call the police.

I can hear through my bedroom window, because this weekly ordeal is just a few feet from it, as Spencer sex-whispers his usual apologies and tries to gather support from Other Single Mom by explaining, literally, the entire nature of their fight and their drama.

Other Single Mom takes the bait, just as I always do.

Or maybe she calculates, as I do, that Spencer looks like the kind of guy who knows people who don't mind breaking and entering and assault and just wags her finger and shushes them and goes back to bed.

At this point, Spencer sex-whispers black Snookie into cooperation and the two go back inside to talk it out. A few hours later I am treated to the sounds of loud, rough makeup sex.

They are my ex-husband and I ten years ago. Exactly. And so I both pity them and hate them.

I'm the One For Me

Well, I will be, soon.

See, one of my dearest friends bestowed a nugget of wisdom upon me about a year back:

BE the man you want to date.

About a year ago, I was working at a hotel as a concierge. There was a guy there who I was very attracted to, and being "separated" I figured a little workplace fling was fair game.

We were teetering right on the edge of Friendship, about to dive right into More Than Friendship when I gushed to my friend, The One Who Usually Has Relationship Issues.

"Girl, he is amazing," I swooned, "We laugh all time. He likes astrophysics just like me. And he is tall. And has a degree and…"

"Jessica. You don't have time for this."

Um...excuse me?

At that point was thinking I needed to find a new friend. I had indulged This Particular Friend through every one of her giddy crushes and relationship roller coasters since we were fifteen and now she can't return the favor? I retorted.

"But girl, I haven't slept with him or anything. Do you hear me? I am attracted to him and I have *not* had *sex* with him. For me, that's kind of big deal!"

"I can't even believe you. You are going on about wanting to date this guy. You need to date yourself! Get dressed up for YOU. Get sexy for YOU. Find out what turns YOU on, not HIM! You have never, ever, ever just ...just been...just you."

WHAAAAAAAAAAAAT!?!?!?

Am I being schooled by The-One-Who-Usually-Has-Relationship-Issues?

Is this some sort of 5th dimension alternate Universe?

She was right.

Holy shit, she was completely right.

I had never been just me. At least not since I got boobs.

Ever since I was twelve or thirteen I always had a boyfriend. And later, when I started having sex I always had a guy I was having sex with who I referred to as my boyfriend.

Then I married the aforementioned guy.

I was barely separated from my husband and I was already trying to latch myself onto another poor fool. What was wrong with me?

What *was* wrong with me? Why *didn't* I just date myself?

I spent a few days rolling it around in my head.

Why *Didn't* I Date Myself?

Well, I think the first problem is I would NEVER date someone like me!

Oops.

But seriously...
I sat down and started listing the must-haves for the next man I decide to let into my world.

He must be fit and attractive. He must be educated, or ambitious or both. He must be stylish. He must be creatively talented.

Hmm....

I am none of the above.

How exactly did I think I was going to land this fit, sexy, stylish, ambitious creative man when we would, clearly, have nothing in common?

And then another revelation.

I can just *be* the man I want to date. Why, in the name of All That Is Holy, am I expecting some dream man to come complete me? My lazy ass don't got that much time! Why the hell not just do it myself??

I took over ten years of French and can't hold a conversation in French. Unacceptable. I was the Student Director of my school's show choir and the SGA Vice President of Fine Arts. I can read music. But I can't play guitar or piano. Unacceptable.

You can only fall back on the old "my Dad wasn't around" schtick for so long before you just look like a lazy-ass whiner.

I had become a lazy-ass whiner, waiting for Mr. Awesome to swoop in and teach me all the things Daddy didn't.

Unacceptable.

I finished my list of everything I wanted in a man. Then next to it, I made a list of how I could develop those traits in myself. Then, in a third column, I added some oddball traits just for me:

I want to be a chick who is good at poker. I want to be more versatile with my hair. I want to speak five languages - at least. I pick them up easily, why the hell not? I want to wear red lipstick, like, every day. I want to learn how to drive a stick, just in case.

However, due to my staggering poverty I was not quite sure how I was going to afford five copies of Rosetta Stone software so I turned to the interweb and *Voila!* I found everything I needed to learn everything I want!

Free Guitar lessons on YouTube, free language buddies via Skype. You can literally learn anything.

But all of those things, while neat party tricks, are topical. What this conversation with my friend really did was force me to deal with my Self.

With everything upended and so logistically difficult I have become near-obsessed with figuring out what in my soul was so parched that I chose *that* man, chose to marry *him*, chose to stay as long as I did and now find myself single with three kids with no education and no job.

About a year ago when I first moved into the apartment, my stepmom offered me the chance to go to one of those spiritual, deal-with-your-issues kind of retreats. I went and did more healing, crying in a room with strangers, than I had in the span of my life. Issues I'd had for as far back as I could remember vanished from my spirit. The whole experience was painful and intense but I loved it because it's so satisfying on the other side and it makes me feel like an emotional archaeologist.

I really like analogies and I thought of this one last night:

Digging deep into your subconscious mind and heart is like digging for bones.
You see something jutting out from somewhere deep, curiously dust it off to reveal it. You didn't know it was there before...and now you do. So you *keep* digging, looking for clues. You know you'll find more.

Eventually you unearth the whole monstrous thing. It's the skeleton of a T-Rex. It's massive but it's not whole so now you have to reassemble it.

You take your time, painstakingly recreating the monster it once was. Only now it is not a terrifying, menacing monster. It is inanimate. It is just a shadow of its formerly life-threatening self. There's nothing scary about it. It is not alive *now*. You are not in danger. You can stand there, with your head right inside the jaws of this once bone-crushing dinosaur – and feel absolutely no threat. You can intellectually respect its former potential to kill but time has destroyed this monster's power.

That is exactly how emotional archeology works.

Things happen in life. Bad Things. If you experience those Bad Things first hand, there is a good chance you have to adopt some sort of emotional shield to protect yourself from complete annihilation. Then you bury the Bad Thing and still carry the shield just in case.

The only way we can drop the shield is to dig and find the bad thing – reassemble it, name it, examine it – and only then we realize that it is no longer a threat. It can no longer hurt us. It's friggin' dead. As a matter of fact, they are all dead. The *threat* is in the past. And I am *here*, in the *present*, safe and alive. I can take the armor off. I can drop the spears. I can drop the shield.

That is why I love doing this emotional work. It's amazing how placid and static your issues can seem when you realize they are no longer doing you harm in the present...except in your own head.

The Hole In The Wall – March 2011

A year later there is still a hole in the wall. One day when he came over, he was doing some sort of goofy zombie walk to make the kids laugh and he tripped over his own limbs and fell into the wall, his shoulder leaving a massive hole.

The kids scolded him, exasperated that we'd just moved in and our space was already soiled. He promised he'd come back and fix it.

But as time passed I no longer saw it. It was just the state of the wall. The kids stopped caring. And it never got fixed.

That's the way it is, isn't it?

He is destructive and we adjust to the chaos until it's so normal we don't even see it.

Red Lipstick

I'd always wanted to be one of those women who wore red lipstick. It seemed powerful and brave and bold and like you didn't have to do much else to be "put together." When I decided I was going to "reinvent" myself after my divorce I made a lot of noise about how I was going to start wearing red lipstick.

Now that I have publicly declared that I am going to start wearing red lipstick all the time, the pressure is on. Many people are curious about my feelings, assuming I am sporting my red lips, and I hate to admit – I have yet to start wearing makeup.

I KNOW! It should be the easiest resolution, right? And yet, I have attached a mountain of excuses not to do it.

"I need to get my eyebrows done first."

"I can't wake up early enough."

Those are my two favorites.

But the strange thing is that I am completely terrified and I am not exactly sure why.

Let me explain my Red Lipstick Theory.

Red lips are synonymous with a lot of things: glamour, power, sex, classic beauty, elegance, Gwen Stefani, Dita Von Teese...

I'd have to say that lately my Self as "Mrs. _____" is *not* synonymous with any of those things.

However, "Jessica Vivian" apparently was.

Case and point, my senior year quote, under my thin and beautiful and glowing and hopeful eighteen-year-old face was:

"When in haste, walk slowly and make sure everyone can see you." —Marilyn Monroe

I. Shit. You. Not.

Seriously NOT the kind of thing a pudgy, mom of three would say but a sexy ass eighteen year old with an ego the size of Kazakhstan? You bet!

But here's the deal:

I'm divorced. My name is no longer hyphenated. I am just "Jessica Vivian" again.

So why don't I feel Jessica Viviany? How do I get that ballsiness back?
I'm gonna start with the Red Lipstick. I capitalize it because it deserves that much reverence.

So here's how it goes, in my head at least:

Red lips are slightly high maintenance and I am trying to dive into the I-give-a-damn-how-I-present-myself-to-the-world lake head first. When one is wearing perfectly lined Red Lipstick, one cannot also wear one's pajamas and house slippers to CVS pharmacy – like I did this afternoon – without looking slightly unstable.

Taking the time to make your lips pretty, means you have to make your face pretty and if you've gone that far, you might as well pick out a decent outfit.

See how that works?

Now, makeup and I have a really spotty past. I wore it to the prom. I wore it at my wedding. I had to wear it when I worked at the shady "modeling school" I was working at when I first met him. I stopped working there about seven years ago.

Since then I have worn it sporadically to work. I usually avoid it because when some well-meaning member of my family happens upon me with my face done they usually make such a big, ridiculous deal about it and fawn over me like I'm an effing show dog with their high-pitched "Oooooooo, don't you look pretty?!"

Gag me.

A few of my friends have said that for them makeup is a mask from the world. I *wish* I felt that kind of solace and safety in it. I feel the exact, polar opposite when I'm wearing makeup. I feel like I am under a spotlight. I feel seen and exposed and vulnerable. I feel like everyone is looking at me, and not in the way I like.

How odd.

I am a hammy stage-hog and I don't mind being the center of attention if I'm cracking jokes but not when people are noticing the way I look. I wonder what that's all about...

Anyway, I feel like I have to push through this blockage.

Nowadays I am beginning to feel that nothing is as simple as "I'm lazy" especially when there is this much resistance. You know how much I love emotional archeology.

So I think Red Lipstick is the key to examining my unwillingness to be seen, my fear of vulnerability, my disdain for being told I'm pretty. And to put even more pressure on myself, I am hereby declaring that once I throw on said Red Lipstick, I will make it my Facebook and Twitter profile pic.

This is a big deal for me because there is not a remotely recent picture of me anywhere on the internet.

Deep breath

Exposure therapy, here I come

Parenthood Is Overrated

Yeah, I said it.

Yeah I got three kids and I STILL SAID IT!

No, but really. I think it's overrated.

I know, as a mom, I am not supposed to say that. But frankly, most days I don't see what the big appeal is. I don't see what the appeal is of a lot of things. Marriage, for one. Parenthood, for another and I've gone and done both.

Now let me sidebar for a minute...

"I'll eat you up I love you so" is quite possibly the most accurate line ever created to describe the primal, obsessive love a mother feels for her children.

I sniff my children, constantly, literally intoxicated by their little dirty sweet stink, each so unique I'm sure I could smell my kids, like a lioness, if I were blindfolded and made to identify them.

Sometimes I look at them and the wind is knocked out of me, I find them so beautiful and so golden. And sometimes, I squeeze them desperately in my lap knowing that one day they won't fit, or they won't want me to hold them telling myself *"remember this size, remember the little hands, remember the feel of the little skinny arms because they won't be here forever."*

That being said: Parenthood is not fun.

How something can cause such feelings of failure and dissatisfaction and simultaneously be everything you live and breathe is completely beyond my comprehension. I'm not sure if there is anything else as maddening.

I've been a mom for eight years. I think I am doing a good job, mostly. But here are some things about parenting I have come to realize.

1) The scariest thing about becoming a parent is not how it changes you, but how it *doesn't*.

People enjoy rhetoric, I've noticed. Some people more than others. It's not hard, here in suburbia, to find a gaggle of ladies saying things like "Parenthood Changes Everything." Well yes, parenthood does change a lot of things but it's doesn't change as many as you would like.

I have always cussed like Sam Kinison - from the time I was about eleven. Terminator 2 came out and little Eddie Furlong with his floppy, 90s hair was the cussin'-est little, scooter-riding bad boy. I thought he was awesome. I started cussing at will. I even remember the group of kids I hung out with in elementary school, all the kids whose moms actually had jobs, who had to stay in after school care - all delighting in this new form of expression I had made available to all of us. It wasn't long before we were all exclaiming "shit!" during dodgeball and calling each other "jackasses" on the monkey bars.

That didn't change as I grew up. And now I have kids and I am a cussing mom.

I don't cuss *at* them, typically, but I cuss around them. And now, they have potty mouths. Case and point:

Child #3, my mini, keeps climbing out of bed with reason after reason to NOT go to bed. Exasperated, I exclaim:

"Young lady, I don't give a damn, you need to get in your bed!"

To which she responded, "I'll give YOU a damn!"

Parenting fail; yet funny nonetheless. And thankfully none of them do it in public or at school and know not to cuss around their conservative family on their father's side...shit, I could only imagine.

So you see.

You're a mom. You still cuss. You still have a short temper, maybe even shorter. Or you are not as active as you said you would be. Kids don't come out and wave a magic wand that completely changes your personality or your husband's. Just FYI.

You're still lazy. He still watches porn. You still smoke. He can still spend six hours playing X-Box. Come to terms with this now.

2) Almost every mom as had an "Angry Mom Dr. Phil Hidden Cam" moment.

It is unnerving watching those shows, with the screaming moms throwing tantrums. But here's what people don't realize:

Sometimes the mommy meltdown is an effective strategic ploy. Here's how I use it:

The kids are fighting like crazy. I have tried every legal discipline strategy imaginable: time outs, quiet corner, writing "I love my sister" 100 times, moving a paper clip on a naughty chart - all that obnoxious, exhausting crap. But still it continues:

"He took my toy!"

"She called me stupid!"

"She hit me first"

"I hate you!"

"I HATE YOU!"

That's when I cue the mommy meltdown. It usually goes like this.

"YOU ROTTEN CHILDREN ARE DRIVING ME UP A GODDAMN WALL!!! EVERYONE GET IN YOUR ROOM! DO. NOT. MAKE. A. SINGLE. SOUND! NOT ONE! NOTHING!!! UNTIL

TOMMORROW!!!"

Then I hear them all gasp and giggle and whisper

Mom has gone mad, they think.

We should do something nice so we can get the hell out of this room, they plot.

Usually at this point, they work together to clean the room to perfection – a love offering to buy their freedom. Mission *doubly* accomplished. The kids are friends again *and* they cleaned their room.

Without chaos there cannot be peace, yes?

3) You don't have time to teach it all but you have to get *clear* about what you *do* want to teach.

My generation, as parents, is inundated with self-help psycho-parenting theories: Tiger Mom Parenting, Attached Parenting, Crunchy Moms, Helicopter Moms, Authoritative Parenting, Permissive Parenting - it goes on and on.

Many parents I know are constantly educating (and berating) themselves on how to be effective, loving, nurturing parents. However, it still seems there are parents out there who are just...doing whatever. Just doing what they feel at that moment, willy-nilly, all the time. I don't really agree with that. Here's what I think:

There are probably 50 qualities you would like to really, deeply, teach your child. Respect, Integrity, Ambition, Love of Nature, Grace under Pressure, etc. But you have *time* to focus on, say, five to ten before they are out on their own. It's as quick as a flash.

You and your partner in parenting have to get a super clear idea of what traits are most important to you and you have to discuss, openly, the Issues that both of you are dragging from your own childhood experiences into your current parenting practices.

Maybe you were given tons of gifts, but no attention growing up. Or maybe you got neither, so you drown your kids with both.

Either way, too many parents simply never discuss it and spend the precious and terrifyingly brief eighteen years they have arguing and second-guessing and squabbling and then poof! The kids are gone and that's one more parched, dysfunctional adult walking around.

It's work. It's hard, hard, hard thankless work. Sometimes it's crazy hard and the hand drawn hearts and love notes aren't cute enough. Sometimes you want to take a nice long bath and let yourself get pulled down the drain, cartoon style - riding that pipe to a new life in a new place.

But you can't.

This is the life you chose. You have to wear it. You force yourself to enjoy it. You learn to find joy in the bad knock-knock jokes and the school plays. But sometimes, when you're not thinking about "the life you could have had" and your guard is down, your son lovingly twirls his fingers in your curly hair, and looks at you with his dreamy gray/brown eyes and says some romantic nonsense like "Mommy, if you died the whole universe would move because everyone would hear my sad love cries."

And then you realize that even though your life is not particularly meaningful to you it's everything to someone else...and sometimes that is enough.

Jesse/Jessica

I actually wore makeup, like, four times this past week so pat me on the back. I'm still having a hard time rectifying the really tomboyish, masculine part of me with the female part of me.

I know what kind of girl I wish I was.

I wish I were the kind of girl who got her nails done, who was smallish and smelled good all the time, who wouldn't think of leaving the house without makeup, who cowered into some alpha-male's side during horror movies. But I am soooooooo not that girl.

I stink most of the time. My nail polish is always chipped. I hardly ever leave the house *with* makeup. And I am pretty sure I have never dated a male who didn't secretly want me to be his mother, forcing me into the position of protector and wound-soother. This wouldn't be such a problem if I actually wanted wounded-artsy-whiner boyfriends but I completely don't!

I like alpha males. A lot.

And girly girls make me seriously uncomfortable. I feel so awkward in groups of women as if I'm doing "being a woman" incorrectly. The whole scene is just awful. I just have a lot of residual masculine energy.

The combination of not having a male authority figure growing up and my marriage to a feminine energy male has caused that part of me to develop – that missing male part – and the rest of me to take a back seat.

If there was a "How to be a Girl" class, I swear I'd take it.

For now I feel like a really brusque, emotionally detached, animalistic, bawdy enigma. Maybe, I'll be able to cultivate it into something really lovely and attractive one day.

Work

I'm not quite sure how I'm supposed to make this work. The cost of after school care for three children is about $900/month. How would I pay that and my rent? Right now we are coasting on the hundred dollars here and there that I get from my ex-husband. We eat a lot of beans. I actually contemplated becoming an escort. I also thought about selling my used panties on EBay...

Things are less than ideal.

Big Fat Liar

I confess. I'm a big fat liar. I *do* want to get married again eventually...I think...

Maybe I just want another wedding - anyone who attended mine can tell you it was a blast.

But I am so scared that no one will ever want to date me so I keep lying and saying I "hate marriage" because "don't get it" and "don't believe in it." But the truth is that I have fantasized my wedding to various fantasy celebrity boyfriends at least a dozen times.

But I have three kids.

THREE!

FUCKING.

THREE!!!

I went out to eat the other day with his mom (I didn't pay for it) to have a delish half sandwich and soup and the little shit-head line cooks were like "Hey, check it out, that girl's hot."

Then another one goes "Pfffft, three kids, man. No way."

OH MY GOD!

Loser-ish line cooks at Random Sandwich Cafe think I have too many kids to be dateable!?!?

NO! NO NO NO NO NO!!!!!

Not! Okay!

NO!

And then there's the other end of the spectrum. Say I meet a guy and he's like "Three kids, wow, no problem. I love kids. I can't wait to meet them."

Then I'll be scared that he's a molester! I mean, this *is* Florida. I would be *so* suspicious of a guy who was okay with my having three kids that I would probably turn him over to the police within minutes.

Ugh, a conundrum.

But apparently, there *are* guys dating single moms.

My single mom friends go on dates. Personally, I don't have time to brush my fuggin' teeth let alone go on a date. Plus I've only been on one that I can remember. The guy hit on me at Barnes and Noble. We talked for hours after he gave me his number. We went to dinner and saw a movie.

Then as he was driving me back to my car I noticed the carseat in the back of his SUV. He had three kids, apparently aged eight, six, and four.

"How old are you?" I finally asked.

"Thirty-seven."

Um...I was fifteen.

Awkward.

And illegal and gross.

I'm lying again, that's not the *only* date I ever went on but it was the first. I think my ex-husband took me out a few times in the beginning.

But then there's that hideous single-parent double standard.

Single dad = *Aww, how sweet, taking time for his kids, dedicated father*

Single mom = *Same ol' shit*

Fuck my life. I think the ideal scenario would be a long distance relationship that spans decades like in Brokeback Mountain. Goin' on "fishin' trips" and making out in the woods and havin' hot, dangerous anal.

(whoa, sorry...got carried away)

But, alas, I think for the next couple of years my only romantic partners will come with batteries.

And another alas, actually, I can't even keep those around because my kids are too damn sneaky and I wouldn't know where to hide one if I had one.

Ugh.

. I miss makin' out.

Sequins and Leopard Print

I was folding clothes with my oldest child, Jaya (rhymes with papaya, not that complicated) and she dropped a knowledge bomb on me:

"Mom, all of your pajamas are really colorful like pinks and oranges and yellows but your, like, real life clothes are all black and gray and dark blue. It's like you're secretly exciting but don't show it."

WHAAAAAAAAAAAAAAAAAAAAAAAAAAAA?!?!?

Ugh, she's right!

Sidebar: Am *I* ever right these days? Seems everyone else is.

In my head I am all sequins and leopard and red and hot pink and punk rock and glam and nose piercing and more tattoos. But on the outside I am Frumpty Dumpty professional mom in discount jeans and a wide variety of black, gray or navy V-neck twofer t-shirts.

Sometimes I get crazy with a flower headband - always in black though. What the hell is that about?

I mean it, I'm not about to say something really deep and inspiring. Seriously, what the mother eff is that about?

I went shopping today to help look for a big girl job. Any job that requires me to actually talk to people and actually wear something other than yoga pants and flip-flops is currently out of my reach. I'm pretty sure I haven't had to wear heels in over a year and I only recently started wearing clothes that weren't workout/pajama hybrids.

Anywho, I went to the Maxx – because that's what broke, er, *frugal* people do – and I got a cool Calvin Klein suit. Then I went shopping for some shoes because I purged myself of all sexy shoes sometime in 2008. I hit the DSW and found some awesome mustard yellow pumps. They were so amazing. They were also in teal.

I didn't buy them. I was afraid to buy them because I knew I'd be too insecure to wear them. Wtf?

Instead I bought some moderately interesting yellow and gray leopard pumps – I know it *sounds* more interesting, but trust – they are not.

Guess what else? I wussed out on the red lipstick, too. I bought several, all of them frightened me. I wear a darkish mauve-ish color on the ONE day a month that I attempt to look older than nineteen. Lame.

So all the balls and gusto and sparkle I *think* I have has apparently fizzled and I am not, at all, closer to putting myself together than I was in Feb when I started this idealistic attempt at reinvention. Buh.

I need a RuPaul's Drag Race drag queen intervention.

A Different Boy – April 2011

My six year old son is a different boy.

He's still snuggly but he's also angry. He hits his little sister and he destroys things. I woke up late at night to find him burning black holes into the carpet of his bedroom with a lighter he'd taken while his father was visiting. He draws all over the walls and cuts his clothes to shreds. Thankfully, at the very least, his behavior at school is okay.

He seems to be saving all the anger for me.

We often end the evening in screaming matches and I dig my nails into my palms to avoid spanking or slapping him.

A few weeks ago he asked to be called by a new name. He picked "Jacky Jake."

"But what's wrong with your name?" I asked.

"I never know when someone is talking to me. Someone calls my name and I come and it turns out they were talking to Daddy or Papa" he answered.

He had a point. He was named after his father and *he* was named after his father and *he* was named after his father.

My son was the fifth with his name as if he was part of a monarchy. I never wanted that to be his name and his father only halfheartedly so but we felt obligated to and obligation is the love currency in his family so like a good daughter-in-law I obliged.

"Okay," I said, "but Jacky Jake is a bit complex. Can we just call you Jack? It's a very strong name. Kind of a hero's name. Or a wily, charming kind of character in a romantic comedy."

He considered it and smiled to himself.

"Okay. I want to be Jack from now on."

He paused and looked me in the eye.

"I really don't want anyone getting me mixed up with Daddy *ever* again."

My son is a different boy.

Mothers Day Lamentation – May 2011

So last week was crazy emotional for me. Specifically, Mother's Day was a complete mind fuck.

This is the first Mother's Day I've experienced as a single mom. My ex-husband never cared about Mother's Day, so it's not like I was missing the attention and affection that most wives experience on Mother's Day. You can't miss what you never had.

But, my ex and I had a really tumultuous week – lots of drama and fussin' and all that as we adjust to our new roles.

Frankly, I really hated him last week. But I can only spend so much time complaining about my ex before a part of my brain says, *"Yeah, but YOU married him."*

The guilt and shame and embarrassment I feel for having wasted the last ten years – all of my twenties – trying to make a miserable, fear-based marriage work sometimes overwhelms me. It became especially acute as Mother's Day approached.

I wouldn't *be* a mom had I not been plagued with terrible self-esteem and an insatiable addiction to male attention. That's nothing to celebrate.

Yes, my kids are amazing and I can look at the last ten years and be thankful for that.

But now that I know what I want, and I have developed standards for what I want in a man – the man I want may not want *me* —because I have three kids and I am forever attached to the person who helped create them.

Let me give you a clear picture of what I am feeling right now. My marriage was something like this:

Let's say I'm on the beach with a friend, and in the distance I see a really beautiful island. In my head, I visualize myself living on that island paradise in a really cute bikini, sipping drinks out of coconuts and basking in the sun. So I start to swim out to it.

My friends warn me,

"Do you have any supplies? What is out there? Do you have bug spray? Is there food? Do you even know how to build a fire? You don't know anything about that island!"

I ignore them. I'm swimming out to that island. It looks awesome.

As I get closer, I realize the island is really dirty. I reach it and can hear the wild cries of unknown animals. It appears there are no fruit bearing trees. I can see snakes and spiders in the brush.

I turn and look back toward the beach I came from.

It's far. I have been swimming for a long time. I'm tired and I'm already here. I figure I'll just hang out for a while, gather my strength and then leave again.

But days turn into weeks and weeks into months and into years. Wild beasts can attack at any moment so I have to be alert, but eventually learn how to protect myself from them. I learn to build fires. I forage for nourishment.

I learn to survive.

I start talking to myself – replacing any needs for actual human interaction. I'm on the verge of losing my sanity.

Now ten years have passed. I have been wearing the same tattered remains of cloth for the entire decade. I am malnourished; a mere shell of who I used to be. I am hardened. I am bruised. I have infected sores. I am *tired* of fighting snakes. I am *tired* of roasting tarantulas for food. I cannot stand one more day on this stupid island. Even if the swim *kills* me, I am going back to the beach I came from.

I swim through the shark-infested waters back to the beach to find my old friends. Everyone is so clean and so plump from food. They have enjoyed full spectrum of the richness of life. They have homes. They have affection. They have clean clothes. They wear shoes.

Suddenly, I feel extremely foolish.

I left civilization for that *bullshit*, for a *fantasy*, and meanwhile, I could have had all this!? What was I thinking!?

Friends answer, "You were really determined to live on that tropical island. We tried to warn you – holy God, you look like shit."

I'm completely dazed. Ten years gone.

I have forgotten how to be among people. I have forgotten how to care about the way I look. I only needed to know how to avoid death. I forgot how to use a fork. I have been so isolated that I am now an alien. I'm unable to understand human interactions, but desperate to experience them and also terrified.

That was my marriage. It was complete hell. But I had been there for so long and had adapted so well I didn't realize quite how bad it was until I left. And it's not some terrible thing that just *happened* to me – like a car accident, or cancer. It's a hell I *chose*. I walked right into it. I signed the papers. I was *at* the party. And I was looking right at it, cringing "shit, that looks pretty treacherous," and still did not turn back from it.

Why?

And then Mother's Day comes around and I know I need to remember that three amazing little souls chose me as their mother and I am so blessed and so honored that I get to have them as my students and teachers for a while. But it's hard to compartmentalize the joy from the shame, and the grieving of the time lost and the things I have given up.

And the things I may never have – like a relationship or marriage based on love and respect; not fear and pride.

I was simply too proud to admit I'd made a mistake. It was an emotionally expensive mistake and I can't get that time back. But anyway, it is Monday I am finally done grieving. I was not at the cookouts or playdates. I spent the week crying in my shower. But then I spent Sunday cleaning out the things I don't need. Removing the items that no longer serve me.

Awkward

Just when you think you're over the hump your ex-husband walks in with a Brazilian woman.

I haven't had a week this emotionally challenging since the garbage can incident.

It all started last Friday when I ran to my kids' grandma's house to drop off the little one to play with her cousins. His car pulls up. Another car pulls up behind. And in it is a tiny, moderately attractive Brazilian woman in yoga gear.

Hmm...

They come in. She is completely unable to make eye contact and he tries to make a combination version of himself and make small talk.

Then the Brazilian asks my daughter *the* most irritating question:

"Can I touch your hair?"

Excellent.

I feel my throat closing and my heart pounding and my cheeks hot.

I leave.

Five to ten minutes later, I am fine.

I rationalize my feelings.

I am not jealous, necessarily.

My ex-husband is in that yoga world. Every woman he meets is going to be much smaller than me and more flexible. I am not even attracted to him anymore. I do not want him back.

But, it's irritating that I put in ten years of drama and another woman might reap the benefits. He might be a better husband to someone else.

As a matter of fact, he probably *will*. The unfairness of it all is disgusting.

Later, when I compulsively asked him about her, he snapped, "you won't approve of anyone I date until you're dating someone."

"No, I won't approve of anyone you date because I am here washing thirty pounds of YOUR KIDS' LAUNDRY, scraping together change and lugging laundry baskets and pissy sheets up and down the stairs, while you get to have the time to date someone just because you're too incompetent to raise the kids yourself."

He accused me of being childish.

I pointed out that if the tables were turned, he'd be just as affected.

He insisted he would not.

Then I did something I am not at all proud of.

I told him I slept with someone else since we've been apart. I will not share whether or not that is true. It was not my finest moment, and that is exactly my point.

He and I still have our hooks in each other and we completely bring out the absolute worst in each other. We have way too many years of resentment and we simply cannot *see* each other. All we see is the last ten years. We see all the insults, all the fights, all the neglect.

When people asked me why I didn't move back home I felt really noble in my answer. He and I "got along well" and it's what's best for the kids.

I think every person getting divorced believes they are the exception to the rule.

We are better than that. No vile courtroom battles for us. How immature!

Fuck that. I wish I'd moved home. I still wish I was back home.

The problem with staying close to your ex is that you are still sewn into their life.

My social circle consists of his mom, his sister, and one of his friends who recently confessed she hooked up with him before she met me.

Fucking outstanding.

And since the largest connecting factor in all three of these friendships is the fact that we are both in *his* life he is often the topic of discussion.

I am sick to death of him. I am sick of talking about him. I am sick of complaining about him. I am sick of seeing him.

My job (oh yeah, I got a job, more on that later) is isolating so I don't meet anyone else.

On one hand, I like having other single-mom friends. On another, I can't handle any more female energy in my life.

Well-meaning female friends with bucket loads of advice about how I should handle him.

Really?

Is that all I am? Kids and him?

Either we talk about kids or we talk about him. Do we not have interests?

It's like blow after blow after blow lately. And the re-ignition of the fact that we still *affect* each other just fueled our most base and demonic selves.

After learning of my possible tryst with someone other than himself, he went into a short depression, unable to focus. I loved it.

Then I asked him about a discipline issue with our son and he pointed out that he thinks it's because I am a bad mom. Ouch.

And funny, I know it's not true. But it still hurts and he knows it. That's why he said it.

And I know that he believes he has the right and freedom to date and sleep with whomever and I don't. Hearing that I possibly slept with someone else would emotionally kill him. That's why I said it.

It's this constant back-and-forth emotional stabbing. We are both highly skilled and well trained.

We lull each other into a false sense of safety. We get a little friendly. We have some laughs. We start to think "oh yeah, we are friends. We can do this."

And then WHAM! Emotional assault. And one of us is left bleeding.

You can almost feel the anger like a disease. He is miserable so he infects me with it. I try to pretend I am not infected so I can trick him into thinking he's gotten away with it and then TAG! You're it!

It's exhausting. And it's boring. The whole thing has gotten so, so boring.

I am not one of these people who likes to roll around in misery. I am ready to move on.

But the community I've created is, like, addicted to it.

I need a vacation.

Homesick

When I first left Mobile, Alabama at eighteen to live in Tampa I could have never predicted that I would want to run back home so much. I am so homesick. I haven't been home in a year.

Usually around the year-away-from-home mark I become so nostalgic it is unbearable.

I may be romanticizing because life is so shitty right now but whatever. I miss my mom and my sister and my grandma. I miss azaleas and oak trees. I miss southern accents and smiling at strangers.

I want to go home.

Rollercoaster – July 2011

I quit.

I just quit.

If I'd taken the time to read a post-divorce self-help book like a normal divorced person I would have probably learned all about the rollercoaster.

One week you're all "BEING SINGLE IS AWESOME! WHY WOULD ANYONE GET MARRIED!?"

The next week you're like "being single sucks, I wanna get married…today…to anyone with a pulse."

There are two Jessicas occupying my thoughts.

There is the one who watches the Bachelorette, cries during romantic comedies and is already planning her next wedding. You know, the *real* one for the *real* marriage – the first was a run-through.

The other keeps reminding sappy Jessica that after the bachelorette party and the wedding – the thing no rom-com ever dares tackle – is the actual *relationship* with another human being.

That part I'm still a little gun-shy about.

It's all so much work – my eyes are literally rolling just thinking about all the damn work. The ego-stroking, the negotiating, the (gulp) compromising. No!!!

Seriously I am shuddering!!!!

For a second I thought I was ready to dip m'toe in the dating pool. I set up accounts on three dating sites. None went well. On the first I met one guy, Zack, who within two weeks was chastising me for not calling when I said I was going to call.

FAIL.

On the second I was contacted by a man whose profile pics were his various mug shots. Aside from that Romeo were the dozens of men who messaged me to find out "what I was lookin' for tonight."

NOPE!

The intelligent matching system over at the third dating website had me regularly matched with men who tighten their belts *below* their asses, pose for pictures crouched down next to their rims and are "lookkn fo dem SeXY Azz biG BoOtyy HoEzz"

What!!? Noooo!!!

So I quit. I just quit. I am officially turning the part of my brain that craves companionship off for the next decade or so.

I hate rollercoasters. I hate feeling hopeful about dating and then remembering that I have three kids and am therefore a single man-repellant. I still have such a long way to go on my own. I have to keep reminding myself what my goals were for this year.

Me

Me

Me

Me

and me.

A lone wolf.

….but I am starting to get lonely..

I think this is the perfect scenario:

Single man, no kids (and therefore no babymama), lives in a different state, flies in once a month for a long weekend, we rent a room on the beach, have awesome hotel sex (because it's always better somewhere other than your bed) and then on Monday I am back to real life. No cleaning up his dishes. No fighting over the remote. I don't really want the whole cake – I just want to lick off the frosting.

There. Solved.

Fear

Single momhood has rendered me androphobic. It is completely irrational. I can step outside myself and recognize intellectually how unhealthy it is. But it's there nonetheless.

At some point in the demise of my marriage, my subconscious decided that if I had not been so obsessed with male attention/acceptance I would not have been in that ridiculous marriage in the first place. And a switch flipped. The pendulum has swung very, very far in the other direction and I am starting to believe I am being controlled by my fear. I have hit a wall and I am at war with myself.

On one hand, I crave human interaction. I miss having people over for dinner. I miss hugs. I miss flirtatious glances. I miss sexual tension. I miss wearing heels and thinking I'm attractive.

On the other hand, there is a constant panic alarm going off.

Men are dangerous! You are all your kids have! Stay away from men! Men will hurt you! Men will try to take you away from your children! You don't need the distractions! Men will suck the life out of you!

Again, intellectually I know this is not true.

One man sucked the life out of me. And I wasn't very "awake" yet so I let it happen.

But I feel like I don't have the time to take a chance on anyone else. My walls are up. Way way up. My fat is a wall. The chunkier I am, the less attractive I am. The less attractive I am, the less likely I am to attract an emotionally manipulative person. Or murderous sociopath person. Or child molester person. Or any person.

I never considered myself an extremist *before* but I am noticing a pattern. I want all the attention, all the men, all the time. Or I want none.

Don't. Even. Look. At. Me.

But I'm a little lonely and isolated. And I need support – really, really bad.

I'm not sure where to go with this or how long it will last. But identifying the problem is the first step, right?

Thankfully, I am going to Mobile soon and my friend, Chris, has become my therapist since I am sure no one on Earth knows me as well as he does. I mean that. Maybe he can help me sort this out.

And Now This Shit

My nine year old had a panic attack.

We were at a birthday party at Chuck E Cheese. She's always been painfully, painfully shy and extremely attached to me. At her first day of daycare, when I was pregnant with her baby sister, she stood at the door for the entire day waiting for me to come back. She didn't eat. She didn't go to the bathroom.

At her brother's fifth birthday party, she locked herself in a tiny closet and refused to come out. My best friend, Chris, sat outside the closet and talked to her through the door.

In school she always gets marks for being "good" but even she confessed to me that "teachers only say that because I don't speak."

She's been in and out of the emergency room with asthma for as long as she's been alive despite my extended breastfeeding and her completely organic toddlerdom. She wet the bed until we moved into the apartment. I always knew she was a tense kid. But for a child to have a panic attack at nine...

We were enjoying one of her cousins' birthdays and when I looked over at her her eyes were huge and glassy. She couldn't breathe and couldn't speak. She eventually squeezed out that she didn't like Chuck E Cheese and we left early.

What is happening?

I can't wait for this trip home. I know the kids will enjoy being near my family and I need a break.

I will find us some counseling when we get back. No nine year old should feel stressed out enough to have a panic attack.

Playing House

My mom was worried I was going to crack.
"I can hear it in your voice!" she'd say.
I *was* going to crack. I was fantasizing jumping off the balcony of my apartment. But then I remembered that it wasn't high enough to kill me, and I'd probably just break my ankle and I don't have health insurance.
So she offered to pay for my gas so I could drive up to Mobile. I coordinated it with Chris's visit to Mobile so we could spend time together. Mom took the kids full time. I left them with her and moved into Chris's house for the week.
It was idyllic.
He was working from home during the day and I slept in.
By eleven or so he'd bring me coffee. I'd curl up on the couch and he in a chair and we'd talk about what we wanted to do that day.
One day we rented the Final Destination movies and watched all of them in order while eating junk food. We then ended up at a dive bar and chatted with the bartender and a random patron about horror films into the wee hours.
Another day we attempted to make homemade pumpkin gnocchi with sage brown butter. They were hard and chewy but we ate them appreciatively. We had toasted pound cake and raspberries for dessert.
Another day we lounged in and around the pool for nearly twelve hours. We napped on floaties. We chatted for hours and some hours we didn't talk at all.

Chris and I met on the playground when I was in 4th grade and he in 3rd. We had no real reason to hit it off, but we did. Our friendship was socially precarious for us from the beginning. The politics of the strange bubble that surrounded our predominately white and wealthy private school were complex. Many kids were raised by black maids who were "like family" but the first likely suspect if little Mary Katherine's pearl necklace went missing. He, with his wealthy family and his membership to the Country Club and his blond hair and blue eyes just wasn't supposed to be friends with me. But he was an outsider, too – a closeted gay kid in the upper class in the Bible belt. We wore our masks during the day and clung to each other at night.
We've been friends through some "serious nasty" and our friendship has barely waned. And here we are now. Two grown ass adults still finding solace in each other. My days with him were refreshing. I felt completely relaxed for the first time in months or maybe even a year. And the kids and my mom enjoyed each other.

I also reconnected with a friend from my childhood named Trey. Our moms were both single mom nurses who traveled for work on the weekends. They threw the two of us together in one of our houses, I guess thinking a 9 year old plus a 9 year old equals an 18 year old.
I'm kidding. They didn't leave us alone for whole weekends at *that* age. But we were often left under the care of another single mom nurse's son who was in his late teens until he was old enough to be bothered by us. I thought I was going to marry him when I grew up. He got in with the wrong crowd and was killed before I could...
But Trey and I bonded easily and quickly, watching *Bill and Ted's Excellent Adventure* on a loop and spending hours on the phone. But we lost touch with each other over the years.
Sidebar: You know how when you are living your life, you subconsciously assume everyone else exists in some suspended reality? In your mind, they look the way they looked the last time you

saw them and their lives are as carefree as they were when you were all seventeen.

I went home to Mobile and sought him out hoping that a few days of lighthearted drinking and shit-talking would salve my wounded, post-divorce soul and puny self-esteem.

I was a little bit wrong. We are adults now. And we have big, adult problems. Our parents are aging. We have horrible exes and horrible custody issues and baby mama drama. Our kids are being attacked and bullied at school. We can't pay our bills. Nothing is lighthearted.

Apparently, while I was away ruining my life and having kids, Trey was doing the same. He was now divorced with three sons and had a highly toxic dynamic with his ex. She called and texted several times during our short date. What started as a victorious night of freedom and bonding turned into the two of us, heads hanging, huddled in the corner of a bar catching each other up on our terrible marriages, fighting tears and holding each other tight.

My own issues have left me so full of holes it's a wonder I can stand, let alone allow three little souls to lean upon me. And as it turns out, people I love are as shaky as I am.

And ironically, therein lies the peace.

When *everyone* is hurting, everyone is open, everyone has room for a little more. ..because we have all been much worse and can keep our perspectives. There is no need for falsehoods or phoniness. We can look each other in the eye and say, "Things suck and I don't know how I get through each day," and we know we are safe to do so. Our vulnerability bonds us.

That's quite priceless.

I'm not looking forward to going back to Tampa

An Unnamed Rage Post

So anyways, it was my passionate goal to home educate 2/3 of my children this year. At the beginning of the summer, it seemed completely feasible. It is something I have always wanted to do but, being a single parent I doubted that it was possible. However, after talking it over with the ex, it seemed like it was something we could do if we joined forces.

My ex actually planted the seed since he had met a crunchy, granola woman who homeschooled. Her child is self-assured, sociable and well-adjusted. He seemed eager to support my endeavors.

Being a single mom, on only my income (because it takes *ages* for Child Support Enforcement to actually "enforce") and his occasional contributions, I needed steady childcare commitment from him so I could still get to work so I could do crazy things like, y'know, keep the lights on. He agreed to show up for me and the kids but this proved to be too complicated and I was forced to re-evaluate my plans for my children.

We decided on only homeschooling the oldest for now, to see how it goes and decided to send my two little kids to the closest public school - a school they had been in before. But alas, since moving into my own apartment - a mile away from where I was previously living - I somehow plopped myself in a new school district and our new public school assignment was for a school a good 30 minutes away. I could spend an hour driving them to school every morning, or put them on a bus and hope my 6 year old could protect my 5 year old from 11 year olds.

Fat chance.

*don't bother giving me your story about how "rode the bus and turned out fine." Kids are different. Schools are different and childless people are oblivious to this fact for the most part - save it.

Add to that the fact that I had just spent $250 on clothes only to find out that our new assigned school is a uniforms-only school. This is terrible.

So, I went with my tail between my legs to the charter school we just left and begged for our spot back.

OK, it wasn't really that dramatic but I had friendshipped up with one of these loudmouth, whistle-blowing, drama loving, soccer mom types last year and I fear her reputation for disruption made me guilty by association. I think the principal thought me to be a troublemaker. But really, I only picked the school because I already had a bunch of uniforms kickin' around the house.

So anyway, all of this driving and school finding and school shopping happened in the first 48 hours after arriving home from Mobile. In and out of a minivan, me and three kids, constantly. And just as I'd settled the school drama with the two babies, and had bought a really awesome curriculum for the oldest, the ex comes to me and says he is unable to watch the kids ...at all. He then suggests I send the oldest back to school also.

I say, "Okay, but all my money is gone, can you pay for more uniforms?"

"No."

Let me point out, this is the day before he is going on his 5th or 6th week-long yoga retreat.

Yeah my blood pressure spiked, too.

Let me also point out that he has given me a whopping $40 of child support this month for our three children.

Let that sink in.

So basically, in May I was set to home educate two of my kids - something I am scary she-wolf passionate about. I began freelancing articles about homeschooling. I become the "Tampa Homeschooling Expert" on local news websites. By August, all of my plans are shattered because one person just...won't step up.

And when I pointed this out he snarled at me "Well YOU'RE the one who wants all this *money*, I have to go *work*!"

Right, because I am buying mink coats with his whopping $40 worth of child support...

Gobsmacked.

I never, EVER thought he'd be this kind of ex-husband.

I am so hurt, angry, irritated, defeated, bitter, ashamed...

The next day I talked to Jaya about our plans. She said she was cool with going back to school. Then later that day she said "actually....I am really pissed. I really wanted to home school I am trying to be nice about it but, seriously, I am pissed."

"Fair enough, Jaya. I am pissed, too," I said. "Let's just do it anyway. Let's just figure it out and make it work and just do it."

I took her to work that afternoon. My boss is super flexible. She asked what my schedule was and with "I can't watch the kids" as my last interaction with my ex-husband and I told her I had no idea. She said, "well just bring Jaya to work with you, she's sweet and very quiet."

AHA!

I mentally flip my horrible marriage the bird!

You. Cannot. Control. My. Life. Any. More.

I. Will. Do. What. The. Hell. I. Want. To. Do.

Period.

Jaya and I officially started today. We did math, reading, creative writing and history. While discussing cave drawings, Jaya became nervous and agitated.

"I'm not grading you right now, Jaya. Just tell me what you *think* about these cave drawings..."

"WOW!" she said, "I keep thinking I'm in school and feeling, like, judged. Why do they do that? Why do they praise one kid right in front of you, making you feel so...wrong?"

"Teaching is a hard job. It's complicated. Teachers can't be all things perfectly for all students. But anyways, that's not what we're doing here yet. We are just discussing and learning and guessing and proving and all that kinda stuff for now."

Then she exhaled and we drew stick figure versions of Confucius and Herodotus on our maps and rolled around laughing on the floor of my office. On the way to pick up the younger kids from school, she drew a cave drawing version of the history of her life - making room for the stick figure births of her two siblings, a stick figure marriage, a stick figure divorce, and a stick figure "Jaya" with giant heart eyeballs ogling a cute stick figure dress because she loves fashion.

And I felt really proud.

And I felt really proud of my often idiotic but sometimes useful defiance.

I am a scary, she-wolf mom and I have never been as passionate about anything in my life more than my passion for raising my children.

I do not take it lightly. Not for a second.

I have my whole life to be "Jessica Vivian." I have a very brief and very finite amount of time to be their mommy and to mold them and create the adults they will become.

And when someone hinders my plans for how I will raise my children I will listen and then politely flip 'em the middle. I do what I want.

Love Languages – August 2011

So we're back in Tampa and Jaya has been to two counseling sessions.

I confidently assumed she would tell the counselor how disappointed she is in her father and the strain of his inconsistency is causing her stress and strife. But that's not what happened.

She told the counselor that she wasn't sure I loved her.

I was flabbergasted.

I started rattling off all the things I do for my kids:

I work this job. I make them this or that for dinner. We go to the park. We go to the Science Museum. I take them swimming. I let them sleep in the bed with me if they want to. My back is aching because of it. I come every Friday to their school assembly. How is this possible?

But the more I thought about it, and imagined myself through her eyes.

Yes I did those things, but I do so unenthusiastically.

I *managed* my kids. I managed their time. I squeezed in the obligatory "fun" but was irritable because the fun was keeping me from the laundry or the bills or some extra sleep.

Through her eyes I had to admit...

I probably didn't look like a loving mom.

Being a conscious parent stings. The truth of her disconnection from me felt like a brick in my stomach.

On the ride home she was chatty and bubbly, for her it was a relief to "get it out" but it was fresh and jarring to me so I wasn't a good conversation partner.

But I decided to change it. I decided to make a conscious effort to plug in.

To be honest, I'm not sure I've ever been present even though I was a stay at home mom for all those years.

I managed events. I managed the schedule. I played with them and cooed at them because they are my babies and I couldn't help it but I wasn't particularly snuggly.

There are times when I rejected snuggles and was too touched-out to deal with it. And here's what I got now: a nervous, insecure daughter who isn't sure I love her.

Well, if I've learned anything from this whole single parenting schtick is that if I get myself into a situation I can get myself out. From now on I vow to treat my children like the souls they are. They are here on a journey just like I am. I don't have the right to disrespect their time on Earth in that way by treating them and their needs like an inconvenience. If I choose to take them to the park, I will not let my mind be at the Laundromat. If I choose to bring them with me to the Laundromat, I will enjoy talking with them at the Laundromat. I will not let my mind worry about dinner. If they want a hug I will relax and accept it and pour as much love as I can muster into them each time. I will not squirm and try to get back to my whatever I was doing.

My kids are resilient and respond quickly to change.

I think she will be okay.

Fail

You can't teach what you don't know. For this reason, I will fail them.

I don't know anything about healthy romantic relationships. Not a thing.

It hurts knowing there is definitely, absolutely something you will *not* teach your child.

As a parent, I feel like I am supposed to do it all. I am supposed to make them completely ready for adulthood.

Stranger danger, unsafe touch, don't play with fire, wear a rubber, don't drink and drive, don't do drugs, clean up after yourself, please and thank you, apologize, make a list, keep your word, question authority, fight for others, eat your greens... I can teach that.

But I can't teach what I don't know and I've never been in love.

Kelley and the Job

Words cannot describe how much I dislike having to talk to other moms in the school environment. That was until Kelley.

I don't quite remember how she and I came to be friends. We had one mutual friend, a sort of edgy, mouthy Tiger mom. We sat near each other at the mandatory-if-your-child-is-attending-the-fancy-math-and-science-charter-school assemblies every Friday morning and the deep sighs of boredom mirrored each other and so poof! We were friends.

Or rather, we were sister wives.

See, Kelley is another single mom. Being slightly older and more established, however, she had a few luxuries that my children and I didn't have...like a pool and a washer and a dryer and a house.

So we teamed up.

When her friend was looking for employees, Kelley recommended me. In no time I started working in a small office, making more than minimum wage and working flexible enough hours that I could still pick the kids up from school and not have to pay for childcare.

I helped Kelley by picking up her boys from school and watching them while she worked at her job as a travel agent. She would buy me dinner. I'd make sure the homework got done.

Very few single moms, I've noticed, are able to make these sorts of arrangements but for Kelley and I it was organic. She absorbed my children and I as if we were family.

Looking back, she saved us.

She saved us.

Alone – September 2011

It's great to have a friend, finally, to connect to who has absolutely nothing to do with my ex-husband. But, upon reflection, if I had to give my thirty years a theme the word "alone" would be at the top of the list.

My single mom was at work, bustin' her ass and working double shifts through eighty percent of my childhood. I was a textbook latchkey kid.

Beginning in first grade I was picked up and dropped off by a variety of random adults related to my mother either by blood or occupation.

When she was the nurse at the county jail various police officers pulled through my school's pickup line to get me. Most I had not seen before the moment they showed up.

They had to say the password for me to get into the car.

"beetlejuice"

And I was brought to the jail to hang with mom until the end of her shift, visiting with inmates and showing them my finger-paintings.

When I was slightly older I was dropped off by random friends' moms.

By age eight I was proficient in the kitchen. I could make spaghetti, brownies, Hamburger

Helper. I did my own laundry. I ironed my uniform. I stayed on the phone with Chris until we both fell asleep and drooled into the receivers. Sometimes we could stay up long enough to catch some softie porn on Cinemax. Of course we had TVs in our rooms. "Red Shoe Diaries" was an early sex education.

Even older still and I wandered the neighborhood with a slightly rough crowd of other lonely girls. We hated each other but that never kept us from gluing ourselves together.
Being alone at home was far less bearable.

Some of us were more lonely than others and fell prey to charismatic men. It wasn't long before one introduced us to her boyfriend who was clearly old enough to be her dad. He was balding.

We were twelve.

High school was no different.

I was never accepted by the unending sea of white kids at school. I was hated by the jealous and confused black kids who didn't understand "why I talk white." I took in every stray - every broken, lonely person I can sink my claws into. I possessed them. I filled my empty house with other parentless kids and we drank. Then that got boring so we chatted online. Then we talked to the people we met online on the phone. Then we invited them over. Then we did irresponsible things.

I had some sick, subconscious agenda that I imagine I must have picked up from all the television because it literally could not have come from anywhere else:

"I need someone to take care of me. Older people take care of younger people. Men take care of women."

There was no one around to stop me. I dated men.

Other girls dated boys. And I dated men.

And I felt very powerful but I was *desperate* for someone to see what I was doing and stop me.

To notice.

To show concern.

It didn't happen.

Then I went to college.

I was confused. I didn't want to be there. I had a hard time relaxing and feeling like myself and finding my place. My need for male attention ruined my friendships.

I was scared and insecure and intimidated and lonely.

I did what lonely girls did.

When I found out was pregnant and I told him he said, "I will take care of you."

It was music to my fucking ears. So I stayed like a puppy waiting for my reward. But he wasn't capable of keeping his promise. So I had a baby in a strange town with a strange, lukewarm family.

Fitting in and being accepted by them felt like playing a game I'd never learned the rules of and frankly didn't even realize I was playing.
So I wasn't informed and wasn't invited.

I stayed in an apartment with a baby. Alone. For two years.

There was no one to talk to. I didn't know anybody. And he spent every available minute away from me and my pathetic, bottomless neediness. I turned off the part of me that needed attention, or affection, or respect, or acknowledgment.

Then I had another baby.

And there was no one there.

And I cried alone in the shower.

And I cut into my skin.

And then I had another baby and we moved to *my* hometown away from the people who only tolerated me. And for a moment, I had a family. I had a job I liked. I had a vast circle of friends. I had my mom. I had my sister. I was happy...

...until I wasn't.

Insecurity seeped into the cracks in our fractured marriage and everything crumbled. He cheated. I wanted out. He took the kids to Tampa to visit and convinced me his family was different and that everything would be different and to give it another try. So I moved back to Tampa.

But I was alone again.

I filed for divorce. I moved into a tiny apartment with a pissy mattress. My three kids and I ate, slept and played on that pissy mattress. I could not cry. I could not fold. I could not shake. I was all there was. They were all looking to me. And I stood there alone. And here I still stand.

And part of me is so proud of my independence and my rough exterior and my giant balls and my reputation. But most of me is just so tired and so lonely.

And I really really need a hug and I need to be able to lean on someone. I need a community. I need an extra pair of hands. I need a fresh set of eyes. I need a fucking high-five at the end of a tumultuous day. I need to....

...move back home.

Logistics

This is what I'm dealing with.

"Homeschooling at work" didn't work. But we tried and I got a taste of it. It was good. It's definitely something I want to do again in the future once life is less...just...when it's less. Jaya is back in the Math and Science school and doing fine.

The job is great. My boss is unbelievable. She lets me clock in after I've dropped off the kids and she lets me leave to pick them up from school. It's part time work but with the cost of after school care my take home pay is actually forty bucks *more* working *part time* than it would be working full time. And I need to take home as much as possible.

Unfortunately, because I work now the Department of Human Resources reduced my food assistance.

And then they decided that since I never had a child support order through the state, because he gives me cash, that I must be lying and now I'm under investigation for food assistance fraud and they just cut me off completely.

This is a major inconvenience.

There is no free lunch at the kids' charter school so I am paying for that in addition to gas, laundry, groceries, school stuff, toiletries, clothes and utilities.

My mom, very graciously, pays my rent. If she didn't I have no idea what I'd do.

But I run out of gas often when I'm running errands. I have to call his dad to help because his work is close. He brings me gas and asks why his son isn't giving me enough money.

Well, my ex-husband is a massage therapist.

After we got divorced he decided to go on a tattoo binge and he inked himself from his neck to his ankles.

He did it all "for trade" but I was still furious because I knew he was severely limiting his marketability as an employee and also any time spent in a tattoo chair is time he *didn't* spend massaging someone for money.

It's indicative of the sorts of subtle sabotages he performed throughout his life to keep people's expectations of him nice and low.

So sure enough, just as expected, the money is no longer rolling in.

The kids are no longer getting those weekend visits.

I asked him to pick up the kids from school once a week so I could work a double shift on those days. If I did that, I could make enough money to get more groceries or pay part of my rent.

That turned out to be too inconvenient for him.

He can't find enough massage work, can't afford the gas to come to north Tampa, and is always "working on it."

So now my time is spent calculating.

I have enough gas for the week but not enough money for laundry. I could do laundry at Kelley's or I could take an extra shift over the weekend. If I don't pay the power bill this month I can stock the pantry. And so on and so on.

A few weeks ago, I assessed a particularly empty pantry and found that all I had was flour, baking powder, bread, frozen peas, an egg, and a quarter stick of butter.

I cried for a bit and then realized I could make pancakes. The peas and bread would have to wait.

They'd be really watery, sad pancakes but poor kids don't have sophisticated palates.

I found enough change around the house to grab a cheap bottle of off brand "syrup" and went to pick the kids up from school.

My youngest asked, as she always does, what was for dinner.

"Hmm...I dunno. How about PANCAAAAAAKES!"

My kids were elated. They were so surprised their taskmaster mom was "letting" them have pancakes for dinner. They had no idea there was no other choice.

The kids happily scarfed their sad, watery pancakes and went to bed thinking I was the coolest mom in Tampa.

We eat chili, beans and rice and pancakes for days and days on a rotating basis with various toppings depending on how much cash I have.

Somehow, amazingly, the kids still think pancakes are delicious. I don't know how long I can keep this up.

Exit Plan

Since my heavenly weekend with Chris in Mobile I've realized the best plan for my kids and I would probably be to move back to Mobile.

Outside of Kelley and one of my ex's sisters I don't have friends or support. In Mobile, I have my mother, sister, grandmother and aunt. I have lifelong friends who were excited to see me and who have been rooting for me from afar through the blog. I cannot earn enough money to support us here without childcare. Moving is just the most rational decision.

It'd be easy to justify staying if my ex was more involved but he is not. When I brought the idea of moving to his attention, he did not argue with me. He did not necessarily *like* the idea but, as with most things that release him from responsibility, he felt it was best. He said he'd be able to focus more on finding work and then spend quality time with us when he came to visit.

I am looking at leaving in March because that is when my lease is up. That is a strange time to pull the kids out of school. I'm not completely convinced I want to put the kids in school in Mobile for just the last few months so I am entertaining the idea of homeschooling just through the end of the year.

To research I decided to join a Mobile homeschooling group on Facebook. The women are so nice and so welcoming and so encouraging and helpful.

There is one woman who I'm really drawn to who I'll call CBL which is short for Crazy Blonde Lady.

CBL is very vocal and opinionated and knowledgeable. Her energy seeps through the screen. She is a powerhouse. She is straightforward and brash but not so much so that it's offensive or off-putting, at least not to me. She's like Ouiser from Steel Magnolias with less hot sauce and more sweet tea.

When explaining why I wanted to move back to Mobile from Tampa (shocking) I just referred her to my blog.

She read a few posts and sent me a PM saying "I'm gonna add you to a secret group."

She added me to her group on Facebook. It was a whole community of women comprised of single moms and other women who'd helped them. Then CBL introduced me to the group as Jessica "the one we gotta get the hell out of Florida."

"Listen," she said, "if you just *get* here. You and your kids WILL be taken care of. You will have clothing. You will have food. Just get here. My passion is women and children...especially mamas. I have a huge network. I know just about everybody in the whole damn town. Most of them just call me 'that crazy blonde lady'. But all of them know I get shit done and I mean what I say."

I don't know why but I believe her.

Numb – December 2011

People ask me how I handle my stress, my ex, my kids and my life without medication.

The truth is I turned my feelings off years ago. I'm terrified that I can never get them back.

It is common for people who are facing distressing circumstances to hear these well-meaning cliches:

When God closes a door He opens a window.

God will never give you more than you can handle.

I'm going to have to respectfully disagree and not because I am religiously unaffiliated. It's because I see people crushed and battered by their lives all the time. There are industries dependent on it. *Klonopin, anyone?*

My life *should* be crushing me.

I am single. Big deal. I have three kids under the age of ten. The cost of after school care negates my ability to work full time so I make jack squat for money. I have no washer and dryer, which seemed like a small issue when I hastily chose this apartment, but that means I have to take three or four laundry baskets (depending on who peed and who spilled and who threw up) down a flight of stairs, load it and my kids into my sexy minivan and spend money that I don't have on doing my laundry at a laundromat. I make just enough money to cover my utilities - no more, sometimes less.

The week I realized all my underwear had holes in them and I decided like a selfish, indulgent, wasteful person to buy new underwear, it put my entire month's budget off and I ended up paying my car insurance late. The same thing happened the next month when I bought shampoo and razors.

I am no longer under investigation by the Department of Human Resources and my food assistance has been restored but since I have a job we get around $400/month. That means I have to feed the four of us for around $13/day.

Not per person.

Altogether.

I have no savings, no life insurance, and no health insurance. All of this should make me upset.

But I don't feel anything.

I can list it and I can look at it from outside myself and say "wow, that seems stressful!" but none of it registers in my body. No elevated pulse. No lump in my throat.

Nothing.

I slipped out of myself years and years ago. Right around the time of that panic attack with the garbage can.

Feelings, I decided, are a nuisance and I don't have time for such a distraction and therefore I am done with them. And that was that. I discarded the ones that don't serve me: anxiety, sadness, despair, desperation, hopelessness, hope, elation, joy, bliss, ecstacy.

I am a robot. I am programmed to care for my children. I am programmed to drive my car. I am programmed to perform my boring job. I am programmed to be pleasant and witty when necessary for the former in-laws. I don't remember how to do anything else. I don't remember how to *feel* anything else.

A woman I know well found out she had cancer - again - for the second time in five years. She was to undergo surgery and endure six months of chemotherapy. When I found out I was pretty unmoved. I was some *sort* of upset. Angry, maybe, but not particularly downtrodden. I was as removed from it as I am everything else.

That scared me (but not really, as I cannot *feel* fear anymore) because I wonder what will have to happen for me to to jump back into my body.

I have been floating a safe distance behind myself for quite some time - letting my body take all the blows and watching from far away, assessing the damage intellectually and clinically and logically.

And trust me, my body shows the damage.

So what if everything gets good again?

What if the clouds part and things are okay? What if I can afford to feed us and have a little left over for cute underwear again? What if I am so far removed that I can't feel *that* either? What if I can't feel the *good* stuff?

I'd like to fall in love at some point. I'm pretty certain I've never experienced it. But I'm worried I won't be able to, because I will still be floating somewhere in the ether, miles away from Earth and touch and breath and pain and hope.

The only time I register feelings is in the evenings with my children.

It's my youngest child's hammy performances and wet kisses. It's in her sparkly eyes and her soft, soft hands and her lisp and her living room performance art.

It's in my son's dreamy long lashes and gray-green eyes and constant rambling. And his delirious, flute-trill of a giggle. It was that giggle the doctor said was probably gas when I pointed out that I was *sure* he was giggling at me when he was 7 weeks old and still cross-eyed.

It's in my oldest child's sideways glances and floppy, scarecrow lankiness and Care Bear cheeks. It's in her one-liners, her giant worried eyes and the gentleness she tries to hide.

With them I feel peace and warmth and calm in the wee hours when I let them stay up late just because I am not ready to tell them goodnight.

I need them, so I know I'm still alive.

The Watcher

Bridget is the eyes in the sky.

My apartment complex is like every other low rate apartment complex. We are all too close together. We hear everything.
But while most of us kept our heads down and hurried to and from our vehicles, Bridget sat calm, cool and idly on her second-story balcony, rocking in her chair, smoking a cigarette and seeing everything.
She is there when I leave to take the kids to school and she is often there when I get home with them at night.
When I hear ruckus in the parking lot, she is still on the balcony, no longer sitting but erected and peering like a meerkat. The next day she'd have a full report and as soon as we left for school, she'd holler down the details and assure us that everything had been handled or warn us if they had not.
She looks like Cyndi Lauper and has the same nasal New York accent. And she was always watching.
She was like a ghetto Gatsby. Everyone knew of her and she threw the most amazing parties that spilled out of her apartment, onto the balcony, the parking lot, the nearby lake and sometimes wandering to the pool beyond the operating hours.
"I've lived here fuh-evuh, whaddathey gonna do?" she'd answer when asked about breaking pool policy on hours of operation.
And sure enough, the apartment manager would usually join the revelry. Bridget is just the boss.
She invited Jack over to play with her son once.

While he was there my ex's mom came by to "spend some time with her grandbabies."

This is usually where she sits in my apartment on her phone, telling people how much she loves her grandbabies only to leave 20 minutes later.

"Where's Jack?" she asked.

"He's playing with a friend."

Bridget hollered from the balcony, minutes later, asking if Jack could stay for dinner.

I hollered yes.

I noticed my ex's mom was disappointed.

I didn't change my mind because my introverted son is rarely interested in interacting with other kids. This was a small miracle.

Later, when Bridget brought Jack back home she said to me "I nevuh see them come help you. Nevuh. They take you all for granted. Jack was having fun and I'm glad he stayed with me f'dinnuh...you know, to *show* her."

Suddenly, I realized Bridget was an ally.

And it wasn't long before I needed her again. This morning, I went to take my morning piss. When I got up and turned around to flush, right on the back of the toilet was one of my no-I-don't-think-so's: a lizard. I froze in panic. I can do a lot of very brave things like, oh, say leave my poisonous marriage with no money, food, furniture, education or job.

But pick up a lizard?

No.

Just no.

So frozen, I holler to Jack to please go to Bridget's apartment and ask her husband to come help me catch this lizard. I knew crazy/hot Spencer was probably asleep and would come with a gun and the other single mom always looked like she didn't want anyone to talk to her.

Shortly after, Bridget's husband, Mark, came by. He called from the kitchen, asking where a cup was so he could catch and release.

He came and did just that. I thanked him. He "any timed" and I took the kids to school.

A few hours later there was a knock at the door. It was Bridget.

She got very near me and spoke in a low voice.

"Listen, I really hope you don't take this the wrong way."

That's never a good start. I nodded for her to continue.

"Mark came back from helpin' you this morning and he was a little upset. He said he looked in yuh pantry and that you guys don't have any food."

I wasn't sure where she was going with this. Oddly, we had more food than we usually do and I told her so. But I hadn't seen our situation from the outside. As long as I could manage a peanut butter sandwich, sometimes on one slice of bread folded over and beverage, we were okay.

"Listen, Jessica, I don't wanna offend you or get in yuh business but it really upset Mark's heart and...I just wanted to ask you. Would it be okay if Mark and I buy ya just a few groceries?"

Tears welled up in my eyes.

I had never experienced anything like this from a stranger...ever.

I'm not ignorant enough to let pride get in the way of my kids being able to have a full belly.

I accepted her offer and sure enough, a few hours later they were filling my pantry with all manner of edible things: Pasta, cheese, milk, applesauce...

It was a much needed break.

She hugged me tight and said "I used to see him come and go all the time. He don't bring his kids no food or nuthin'?"

"He does sometimes and he gives us a hundred dollars here and there," I trailed off.

"A HUNDRED DOLLARS HERE AND THERE!? Nuh uh, ain't gonna cut it. I *see* how he is now. He and the rest of 'em. You know, Jessica. I see everything that's going on."

You do, Bridget. Thank God, you do.

Sugar

I don't miss sex. I don't miss dating. But I can't remember the last time I was good and kissed. And lately it's all I can think about.

I used to consider myself to be an unnaturally hot-blooded woman. I was the "Samantha," if you will, among my group of friends.

I was guiding my girlfriends through their personal sexual freedom as young as 17. I had a book about the Kama Sutra in my trunk and stayed up late every night, hoping to catch an episode of Real Sex on HBO. I purchased my first *ahem* personal massager somewhere between my 11th and 12th grades.

College was no different. I worked part time as a phone sex operator which is way less interesting and sexy than it sounds. When I was a lonely housewife I wrote smutty short stories for various erotica websites. Sex was the glue that held my marriage together as long as it did.

Sex, as it turned out, was a huge part of its demise.

But sex complicates things. And once you have sex with someone you are "having sex with them." You can't really go back to *not* having sex. Or *I* can't anyway.

And to get to the sex part, you have to make yourself attractive and actually *talk* to someone else. I really want no part in that.

And I don't really miss sex enough to do something stupid and crazy like answer a creepy Craigslist ad. Plus I'm not keen on being murdered, so I've just forgotten sex altogether.

I don't miss it. I don't care about having it. The whole operation just seems like more work than I'm willing to do. However, I really, really, really, really, really, miss making out. That long, deep, drugging kind of making out that made the tips of your ears tingle and your pulse race and all that...

The kind that didn't lead anywhere – just sugar for sugar's sake.

I'm so out of practice with the whole flirting and kissing and boy/girl thing that I feel like I need a practice dummy. I need a good male friend who will make out with me, not try to get to 2nd base, and not want to bother me with feelings or dating.

Oh well, it's almost Christmas so I'll just add it to my Christmas list.

Wired – January 2012

Despite the current trend of the "sensitive, hands-on, hipster dad" it seems that dads, on the whole, are still taking a hands-off approach to child-rearing. I haven't decided yet whether or not I think this is a bad thing.

"I'm not wired for this" is a common response most of my girlfriends get from their significant others regarding taking a more proactive role in child care.

Here's an example of this hated phrase in action:

My kids attend a school which required 20 hours of parent volunteer activity per year. Now, we know I did not spontaneously produce my offspring alone like some sort of asexual amoeba. I am not the only parent. And yet, when I went to sign the kids up and I asked my ex how many hours he thought he would be able to volunteer at the school he said, "uh, nope...I'm probably not gonna be able to do that. I'm just not wired for that kind of stuff."

Um, and I am???

I never wanted kids!

I thought I'd be hot and single forever. But I was lonely and insecure and fertile instead and so I have three children. And because I had children I learned to take care of them, and I put my needs and personal desires on the shelf to just handle muh-fuggin business. I volunteer at the damn school.

That's what you *do*. I had never even *held* a baby before my oldest was born. Now I'm like the child whisperer.

It was the same for Kelley.

She and I went to the school every Friday morning, reluctantly, and sat through assembly listening to kids read book reports and sing songs in Chinese. We listened to the principal's soapbox speeches. Our asses went numb on child-sized bleachers. It bored the living shit out of us. We could have been in bed. We could have been out enjoying coffee and catching up. But we were there because we *had* to be. We had kids and it's just what you *have* to do.

Now, some would say "Well, then you should *make* the dads participate. You enable them by allowing them to be deadbeats."

Well, yes and no.

Yes, I know I am probably guilty of enabling. I *also* know you can't squeeze blood from a rock and nagging someone into submission is just not worth it.

My friend's ex-hubby typically "hangs out" with the kids by sitting in the room with them and watching TV. My ex, while delightful and surprisingly hands-on in some respects, frequently comes to "see the kids" and ends up eating my food, using my computer and then falling asleep on my couch.

I would like to think that we, as a society, have done a pretty good job of keeping our expectations low when it comes to the male role in child rearing. Turn on almost any television show or commercial and what do you see?

Stupid, bumbling, overweight dads who love their TVs and their football. Hot, skinny wives who love yogurt and hate their bodies while condescending to and cleaning up after aforementioned loser husbands. I mean, seriously, have you seen the commercial where the idiot dad doesn't know how to clean up spilled yogurt and the exasperated wife pantomimes instructions from beneath the glass table while the completely overwhelmed husband smears the spilled dairy product all over while the toddler looks on and laughs at him?

Men are not so stupid, but making them *look* stupid sells yogurt and vacuums and paper towels. Jesus, those paper towel ad execs *love* a stupid, messy husband, don't they? And making men look stupid gives them a little wiggle room. Some of them don't want to do the work, so they feign incompetence, and we pick up the slack.

Then we are stress eating which leads to (AHA!) self-loathing and yogurt. Look at how that works.

It seems I've traveled way off topic here.

<recalculating>

I mean, deep down, many moms think they know better and micro-manage dads until they are close to self-mutilation - or at least that what I see in my everyday socializing. So should we just let dad pop in and do what he *is* "wired to do," whatever that looks like?

I mean, I am a single mom.

Is it fair that I break up *all* the fights, do *all* the laundry, *all* the grocery shopping, have the dirty house, *never* go *anywhere* alone, sit through the horrible children's movies, help with all the homework, clean all the barf and never get laid?

No.

But when were we told life was fair?
Never.

And guess what I get in return for all that crap?

I get *all* the snuggles, *all* the love notes, *all* the giggles, *all* the living room dance parties, *all* the "spin 'til you fall down," *all* the trust, *all* the respect, and *all* the memories.

That seems like a good deal to me.

Punished

That's what it feels like. Deep down. Behind the smiles and hugs and small talk.

I feel – no – I *know* I am being punished.

That's why I locked my feelings away, because every time I feel crazy things like "hope" the Universe makes good and sure to knock it right out of me.

I had a plan. I had an escape strategy. I was going to get the hell out of this town. I was going to finally find a home, plant some roots and watch them grow. My family has had to move something like eight times in five years.

In the partnership between my ex-husband and I, one of us is not very good at accepting responsibility - particularly with finances.

I thought that by *removing* that part of the equation things would change. Nothing has changed. Everything has gotten much much worse.

I was dealt a blow today that nearly took me out. Getting out of my lease a little early to move into the place I found in Mobile is going to cost me a fortune that I do not have.

All my plans are now, again, up in the air. And the staggering cost of childcare coupled with the fact that I didn't finish college places me in a demographic that makes me want to vomit.

Single, uneducated mom with three kids.

Gross.

And the fact that I *still* can't get my feet under me, and that I have to rethink the plan *again,* and that incredibly poor choices I made *over a decade ago* are still poisoning my life are enough to make me think really, really, really dark thoughts. And fight really, really, really dark demons.

I have to shut any and all thoughts of my general failure as an adult out, because the tiniest drop leads to the bowling ball in my throat, and the quivering words and the thoughts of knives and razors. Just being honest. I apologize if I'm getting too scary. I was a cutter, once, many years ago before postpartum depression was a widely known thing. But then, I only had one child and one baby and their eyes and ears weren't so big. For now I just have to hold it. There is no escape.

This is my punishment.

And every *single* day through every *single* struggle – arguing with the Department of Children and Families, asking my ex-father-in-law for gas money so I can get to work, sitting in those disgusting government clinics waiting for up to five hours to deal with these new and interesting ailments that have cropped up – all I can think is that I am being punished. And I fight and fight but eventually I go down the list:

I should never have left Mobile. I didn't even want to go to college.
I should never have introduced myself.
I should have dumped him the first time he cheated.
I should have moved back home when I found out I was pregnant.
I should not have married him.
I should have divorced him sooner.
I should have known you can't help people who don't want to be helped.
We should *never* have moved back to Tampa together.
I should have moved back to Mobile as *soon* as I moved out on my own.

I don't trust my judgment at all anymore; not with men, not with life.
I just give up.

I know "this too shall pass" and I "shouldn't look back" and "I'm the captain of my soul." I don't need any well-wishing. I am tired of it. It isn't working.

I cannot hear or believe any of it right now because I put it in action, take it to heart, and I am still living in an elephant shit sandwich. I screwed up my life. I screwed it bad.

P.S. No need to put me on suicide watch. *He* would get the kids and that would be the real tragedy, trust me.

Crazy - February 2011

He apparently started a relationship with some woman he met at one of the many yoga retreats he goes to.

She is flying to Tampa from Philadelphia to visit and he intends on introducing her to me and the kids.

My first response was a firm "no thanks" which was met with a guilt trip about how *of course* I have a problem with him dating and of course I'm using the kids against him.

I didn't think that was what I was doing.

I admit it pisses me off that he has the luxury of pursuing a new relationship but doesn't feel the same tug to *work* for a living.

We are still trying to move away. I don't feel like the kids need to be invested in his random girlfriend.

He pushed and pushed and guilted and, second guessing my own judgment, I gave in.

Her visit, incidentally, was to coincide with my 30th birthday. Salt in the wound. I decided to call my dad for advice.

My parents were excellent at being divorced. I was two when they split so I actually have no recollection of them as a couple. It didn't matter, though, because they co-parented well enough to take me on a vacation to Disney World together several years later. My parents were always able to be in a room together and make small talk. When they both got remarried, they had already set the stage for the step-parents so then the four of them could be in a room together interacting easily.

When I moved into my college dorm, both my moms were decorating while my dads set up my computer.

"Who are the parents?" my roommate's parent asked.

"Uh...all of us," they would answer.

If anyone could guide me through this new phase of single parenthood, it's him.

I set the kids up with snacks and a movie and went down to my car in the parking lot so they couldn't overhear my conversation. I explained the situation to my dad. He listened intently and then answered.

"Jessie, unless he is planning on getting married, you have no obligation to meet some girl he's screwing. If it's serious, then yeah you're going to have to meet who's going to be spending time with your kids. But if that's *not* what's going on, then *later* for it. As for the kids, you really have no control over that. He's going to date and he's going to want to do the look-I'm-a-dad act on these women because it works. And it might hurt your feelings, but it is what it is."

"Thanks, Dad. I didn't feel okay with it. I can't explain why. I just didn't like the idea," I explained, "I just *didn't*. And he kept telling me I was being irrational and I guess he's right."

"Hooooold on, hold on, hold it, hold it, hold, hold, hooooooold it," he interrupted.

"Jessie, listen to me. If you never listen to me ever again for the rest of your natural born life listen to me now."

I waited.

"You have every right to be as irrational as you need to be. You just got divorced. You are raising kids on your own with no damn help from his sorry ass. Uh yeah, you're gonna be a little emotional and irrational. *Fair*, Jessie. You earned it."

At this point I was fighting tears.

"This whole thing, Jess, is painful. It...it just really sucks. *Let* it hurt. Give yourself room to be a little crazy. You take good care of those kids. As long as you don't drag *them* into the crazy with you, it's fine. So screw him, Jess. You don't need to meet this woman and you really don't owe him an explanation."

Dad is right.

Dirty Thirty

I felt like I deserved to have a shitty thirtieth birthday.

If anyone had given too much of a effort, I would have felt bad about leaving.

I ironed out the kinks in my exit plan and I'm moving next month for better or for worse. I planned on spending my 30th birthday packing and preparing to leave.

My ex called, however, and told me to get lost for an hour because he was on his way with a surprise. I did and when I came back to my apartment there were balloons outside. I walked in to find even more balloons and an immediate dousing in that crazy spray-can foamy string.

It was a sweet gesture.

"I had to do *something* for you for your birthday, especially with you leaving and all," he grinned sheepishly.

I wasn't particularly moved by the attempt because it was only the second birthday of mine he'd ever acknowledged, but was grateful that he included the kids.

He made dinner. I don't remember what it was because he also brought a bottle of wine and I drank most of it. It was *my* birthday wine after all. It was the wine that made me think, "*I should have sex with him, since I'm leaving and all."*

And after the kids went to bed. I did.

And it was sufficient, I guess. I was too hazy to be present.

I noticed that he was making himself very comfortable in my bed, which was strange because I *thought* that perhaps his girlfriend was still in town so I asked.

"She is," he said, matter-of-fact as he readied himself to sleep. That sobered me right up.

What the fuck was I doing? I don't *want* this guy. I don't want him back. But I felt some sort of sick, twisted power in the fact that he left her somewhere and spent the day with me and the kids.

At first I felt like I'd won.

But then I thought about the fact that this woman felt enough about him to fly here to visit. And I thought about how much he lied to *me* and slept with women behind *my* back. And now I was the woman behind her back. Then I felt like I'd lost. I felt super gross and super guilty.

I kicked him out and debated contacting her and letting her know. I knew *he* wouldn't. Their relationship wasn't my business. But I felt some sort of moral obligation to warn her that he was a damaged man who would take her down with him if he let her.

Chris advised me to mind my business. I ignored him and wrote her anyway.

I knew her name because he'd told me in passing and I'd Facebook-stalked her. I wrote the most honest email I've ever written:

Hey, so...I'm his ex-wife and I'm a horrible person. He spent the day with me for my birthday and I slept with him. I am only telling you this because I feel so much guilt and shame and I can't believe I disrespected another woman in this way. I know you spent your money to fly here and it was dismissive enough of him to leave you alone all day. I feel disgusting for taking part in it. I'm sorry. I don't want to come off as a scorned ex-wife or a cock-blocker but, without knowing you I can still tell you that you deserve better than that...

Again I'm sorry.

Sincerely,
Jessica

Shortly after, I received a response but, afraid to read the wrath on the other end of the conversation, I deleted it and blocked her.

Later that day she left a comment on my blog saying she'd read the message and wasn't angry and for me to please email her so we could talk.

I did.

She shared with me that, indeed, she cared deeply for him to have traveled so far. As a matter of fact, she thought she was coming to meet me and the kids because she *did* think that she was going to be a step-mom.

However, upon arrival, she noticed that he was different. He was neglectful and, in her words, "obsessed" with me. I told her that was unexpected as he didn't spend much time with his kids anymore and didn't send any child support anymore. She said he didn't talk about the kids much but he spent a lot of time lamenting the loss of the marriage.

I should have felt some sort of satisfaction in this but really I just felt sad for him.

The entire trip, ultimately, only served to show her that she has problems with attachment. She said she'd been in treatment for Love and Sex Addiction before and this experience inspired her to go back to meetings and get her boundaries and standards together. She even suggested I find some groups when I move to Mobile. I said I'd look into it.

We ended the conversation wishing each other well in our future and vowing never to give him any part of our hearts or bodies ever again.

It was, by far, the shittiest and most awkward birthday I've ever had and just the sour taste needed to shut the door on Tampa once and for all.

The Wendy Syndrome

I'm Wendy.

This particular round of emotional archeology started innocently enough.

My oldest and I were watching the 2003 live-action version of Peter Pan. Typically, PG-rated children's movies based on early 20th century books should not create physical manifestations of anxiety in one's body. But there I was, watching aghast, palms sweaty, experiencing a myriad of emotions I couldn't explain.

OK, Self, time to pull out the picks and shovels.

Later that week, Kelley was razzing me over my bizarre attraction to Chef Gordon Ramsay.

"Ewwww! You think Gordon Ramsay is sexy!? He looks and acts like some bad little boy!"

I think I found something!

And later that week I had a discussion with my ex-husband that made it very clear to me that I was dealing with a boy who refuses to grow up. He is textbook "Peter Pan complex."

If he's Peter then I am most definitely Wendy.

Oh goody.

I looked up "Wendy Syndrome" on the inter webs and learned that there is little about it but the descriptions of Peter/Wendy dynamics in relationships pointed to men treating their wives like mothers and wives using their husbands as protection from their own taboos or negative impulses.

Here it is. An emotional brontosaurus to dig up and assemble.

I'm sure I have never seen a more accurate description of mine and Johnny's marriage. And all the players were present. My living room had a diverse and constantly rotating tribe of Lost Boys, in the form of drinking buddies and other addicts, and he "adventured" with fair share of Tiger Lily's and Tinkerbells (six or seven while we were married, that I know of) and while *my* Peter Pan was out fighting battles and having adventures (in bars and concerts and yoga retreats) I was at home crying, fretting, fussing, doting and playing mom - to everyone.

But don't feel sorry for me. I don't. Apparently, that is what I wanted.

I believe people only do things that work for them - even dark, sad, harmful things. I have always wanted *that* guy. That untamed, over-confident, feral, playfully wild guy. I have never wanted the chivalrous giver/protector/provider.

On the surface I do, but deep down, no. But why?

I am close to the answer but more on that later. For now, let's talk about this Peter/Wendy dynamic.

To understand Wendy we must first understand Peter.

Men displaying Peter Pan tendencies have an inability to cope with what they perceive to be the perils of "the real world" and, namely, adulthood. These men tend to glorify adolescence and cling desperately to that state of entitlement and egocentricity.

To do this, a Peter needs a Wendy to handle all of the adult aspects of his life. Women who take on the "Wendy" role are often multifaceted, but Peter doesn't notice or care. Once his Wendy has been designated, she is never anything *other* than a loyal caretaker from his perspective, not unlike the way some adult children struggle to see their mothers as women.

Wendy replaces the "mother" and Peter ping-pongs between his feelings of devotion and reverence toward her and his urge to rebel against her in displays resentment and false independence. For Peter, as long as there is a wild, earthy woman, a destructive, adventurous peer group to play with (Tink and the boys) and a civilized voice of reason holding down the fort at home (Wendy) then all is right in the world.

Eventually, however, Wendy grows tired of her maternal role and his narcissism and wonders if her Peter is capable of giving more. When he can't give her a straight answer, she moodily retreats.

I recognize this classic Wendy-style emotional manipulation. I was a master.

This is the dance Peter and Wendy perform day after day, year after miserable year. Wendy is using the ol' magnetic "opposites attract" routine. When Wendy withdraws, Peter feels two things: guilt from hurting the woman who obediently cares for him while he disregards her feelings, and panic, because he knows he is completely incapable of taking care of himself.

Unable to cope with his feelings, Peter angrily storms away only to be so overcome by his feelings of insecurity that he runs back to the arms of his Wendy. She is now sated, reaffirmed and knows her place in his heart. And also fully aware of the control she has over his emotions.

But why did I become Wendy and choose suffer all that neglect and drama in the first place?

But there is a little-known, secret side of us "Wendy girls." It is a dark, vengeful, dangerous side.

In the Peter Pan tale, Wendy is fond of telling pirate stories to her two younger siblings - much to her parent's dismay. In their eyes, it is time for Wendy to start acting like a young lady and the night Peter steals her was to be her last night sharing a room with her brothers – no more pirate tales, no more playing pretend.

Peter Pan seems such a convenient and well-timed form of escapism now, doesn't he?

Mom and Dad want me to be a woman but this cute, flying dude says there are pirates and mermaids in his 'hood? SOLD!

Of course, Peter never meant that *she'd* get to hang out with pirates. He needed a mom figure to tell stories to him and his boys. It's a bait and switch I know well. Remember that pirate tales were Wendy's favorite and pirates are cunning, crafty, violent. Fantasizing about Captain Hook offers Wendy something Peter and her parents could *never* give her – true adventure and a taste of danger.

So what's this have to do with my Wendy complex?

Pretty much everything.

I met my ex when I was 19 years old. I had just "taken a break" from college. I put it in quotations because the truth is that I wanted nothing to do with college. I hated it. I didn't want to be there. I worked at Urban Outfitters and at a skeevy modeling school. I had a roommate and we lived in Ybor City - Tampa's version of Bourbon Street. I remember having this near constant feeling of "I don't want to be here."

I know now that "here" was adulthood. I wasn't ready. I just didn't want to.

My ex wasn't exactly a "put together" person when I met him. Actually, he was the extreme opposite of put together. But I think that, subconsciously, I knew that the only way I was *ever* going to "grow up" was through outside force. I would never *choose* to. Something was going to have to *make* me.

My "forbidden impulses" included laying around, drinking and a lot of other things involving men. Hitching myself to someone *more* impulsive let me live out the full reality of those forbidden impulses without actually *experiencing* them. He took the hits for me. He had the "fun."

But he's not happy. He has indulged nearly every impulse that has been presented to him. I was able to see what would have happened if I had indulged my impulses, too. In a way, I used my ex to protect me from myself - my destructive self, my shadow.

And there was a time in our marriage when I took to a life of "piracy." I had my own Captain Hook. I became "Red-Handed Jess."

I had three children in five years, so the years between 20 and 25 were spent breastfeeding, changing diapers, and calling my husband at three in the morning, telling him to come home or else. My life was not mine. My dreams, goals, thoughts did not matter. I was dealing with three children at their most needy and volatile and a husband with addiction issues.

At 25, I finally poked my head out of the laundry pile and got a job. It was quite a bit like stepping on the pirate ship.

Once I got the teeniest, tiny-winy taste of freedom and debauchery I went all the way. Those after work, coworker bonding trips to the bar became nightly events. Many things that my tamed "Wendy" side thought were just irresponsible and childish and rude, Red Handed Jess was out doing with absolutely no conscience. I was not so different from my ex after all.

My version of Captain Hook was man's man with hair on his chest who pretended he was my boyfriend when creepy guys leered. He spent time with my husband to calm any jealousy and promised him he was no snake in the grass. He drove me home when I was too drunk. He always bought the drinks and he never tried to take advantage of my drunkenness. He never wanted me to be his mom.

I thought my ex-husband would understand that it was finally "my time" to be a girl in her 20s and be supportive and hold down the fort at home for once, but it didn't work out like that. But for a little while I got to feel cared for and protected while I indulged...even if it was by someone else.

But ultimately, Captain Hook and Peter Pan are both playing pretend at love. When I started spending more time at home, trying to appease my Peter - my Captain Hook ignored and replaced me. This is right around the time of the garbage can panic attack so I knew it was time to make a choice and, as it turns out, mine and Wendy's choice was the same.

Peter taught her how to fly and offered her solace from societal pressures. Hook let her indulge in her darkest fantasies. But who did Wendy choose in the end?

Herself.

And that's why now, finally, my Wendy complex has paid off.

I choose myself, too.

You see, Peter Pan is not the hero in the story named after him. And my ex-husband, similarly, is no hero in my story. The hero is the one who grows, shifts, changes, realizes something. Peter wasn't willing to grow or shift. He feared adulthood and responsibility more than he feared death. In the end of Peter's story, Wendy goes back to the real world to grow up. She will take the risk. The lost boys decide to go with her, realizing they don't want to live a loveless life. Captain Hook is dead.

Peter Pan just lost *everything*. The family he created left him and his favorite enemy slain.

All he has left is his fairy, Tinkerbell, the only one who doesn't realize she's being used. The only one who continues to indulge him – who still idolizes him. There is no one to fight. There is no woman to care for him. There is no one left to play with.

He goes home to an empty Neverland.

Peter and my ex were unwilling to make sacrifices. They both do what they want to do. They both, ultimately, alienate people.

Like Wendy, I choose to just go home and grow up. I am leaving Tampa for Mobile today.

Like Wendy, my attempt at stalling adulthood backfired.

Like Wendy, I will not waste another moment on flying boys who want me to play mommy. I would rather take on all this responsibility alone with the whisper of a chance that I will eventually fall in *real* love.

I mean, I could fall flat on my face.

But all of that would be better than playing pretend.

Mobile

Move – March 2012

So, I got the eff outta there. I'm moved into a three bedroom house, sight unseen. My totally dope mom checked it out for me and handled all the business end. Transactions are still practically spit-handshakes in Mobile. The landlords liked her so they, by default, like me and my three kids. My mom is good PR.

Kelley called me the morning of the move because she had something for me. It was mattresses.
She just *gave* me three mattresses.
She said a friend of hers was getting rid of them and she knew I could use them.
Who does that?
I don't think I've ever experienced kindness and sistership like the kind I got from Kelley. I don't know if I will ever be in a position to pay her back for her unconditional love. She just *saw* me. She just saw me and gave me help.

Like Bridget.
I can't move away and fail. If I can't pay them back, I at least owe them my functionality.
As for my ex, he was astoundingly supportive. He insisted on helping us move because it'd be better for the kids to see their Dad as part of the process rather than us "leaving Dad behind." He was right. It was good plan.
But I knew things were too good to be true. And he has a compulsion to sabotage good times. Sure enough, as we were packing, we disagreed about something. He threw a fit and said he wasn't going to help me move. Some shift had taken place within me and I just didn't care. I let him leave and called his sister's husband, who was on standby because of my ex's tendency to tantrum out of things, and he said he'd help me move.
Minutes later, after pacing and waiting for me to call him and beg him to help me to no avail, my ex came back and said he'd help for the kids' sake.
Fine.
Shortly after that, all was back to normal. We had a pleasant trip up. He helped us move things into our new place. The kids were completely bonkers bananas at the fact that they could run around in an actual yard. And be as loud as they want without the bang bang, which was a signal to shut up, against the wall from The Other Single Mom back in the apartment complex in Tampa.
We took my ex-husband to the bus station and off he went.
I was free.

I was really free.

Feeling Alone Again – April 2012

I've been in Mobile about a month and my day-to-day has mellowed considerably. Yet despite being in a town where I have so much history, I feel overwhelmingly alone.

I do not thrive in solitude.

I admire people who do. Y'know, like those people who jog and take a sculpting class and read a book and go have coffee alone? That's impressive.

I can tell I'm going through one of those post-divorce phases they catalog in self-help books. This must be the Overcome By Loneliness phase. There are fleeting moments when I think I want a boyfriend. And I think it is at that moment when many of my single parent cohorts actually start dating.

But I am an investigator. I am more apt to examine my feelings than act on them.

And if I ever have some sort of psychotic break where I think I would actually ever want to get married again I want to be sure I am not jumping into the relationship as some sort of salve for my heartache. Divorce rates for first marriages are high, and higher still for second or third marriages.

I guess the simple answer to my loneliness is that humans are pack animals. At least I think we are. We like belonging to groups. We like connecting.

But the reason *my* loneliness hits me like a suffocating vice around my chest is probably due to Solitude being the biggest theme of my life thus far. And Solitude is the catalyst for every negative and life-altering mistake I've ever made. I don't trust myself alone. I don't trust myself anymore *generally,* but especially not alone.

Chris and I were commiserating over our mutual parentless childhoods and the subsequent effects. He reacted by becoming a high-maintenance need-machine. I did the opposite. I am a serial nurturer always choosing the broken misfits as my comrades. Because if I am caring for someone then I cannot be alone.

Both Chris and I, when left alone, turn into uselessness. I stare at walls. I don't eat. I don't want to make the mess or go through the trouble of cooking. It's just me...

It's *just* me...?

And there it is. I typed it and I didn't even know that was how I felt. I'm not worth the effort to me. That's what it all boils down to. Damn, subconscious.

If in my Solitude I do not feel I am worth the effort of basic self-care, then how could I possibly land in a healthy relationship if I choose to seek one?

Any man I meet would be coming in with a job to do.

Give me a reason to care about myself. Prove to me that I matter.

That's a lot of pressure. I would never do that to someone consciously. And now that I am conscious of it I have to just sit in Alone until it feels okay.

The *easy* solution to this loneliness problem would be to just go out and meet people, but I fear my 10 year relationship to an addict has left me feeling quite small and socially inept. Plus, I have three kids with me all the time. It's just easier not to. I'm way too insecure right now. I'm always worried that other breeders are judging my parenting. Then I worry that people without kids think I'm lame for breeding. Then I worry that people think I am a teen mom because I look 19. Then I worry that I dress too young for my age. Then I start feeling sorry for myself because I am poor and only have two pairs of jeans. Then I am depressed because I have fifteen pairs of pajama bottoms. And at that point I am content with playing with bubbles with my kids in my backyard.

So for now, since it makes me so uncomfortable, I will sit with Loneliness and we will get to know each other better.

Naked

We separated almost a year before we got divorced so I've been single for almost two years. I wonder how I will know when I'm ready to date and I keep coming up with one tiny problem.

Someone new will eventually see me naked.

A shocking secret I've learned about a lot of divorced couples, including myself and my ex, is that they still sleep together if they can. Almost everyone I know who has gotten divorced continued to sleep with their ex - some for years after the marriage ended.

I mean, getting laid takes effort and crappy marriage puts you way out of practice. Sleeping with the person you've been sexing for a decade is just convenient. They already know what you like. Or totally don't. But at least you know what you're getting.

I, like so many other moms, have "let myself go." When I only had one child, I smugly watched the weepy doormat moms on Oprah and berated them from my couch.

I will NEVER let myself go! You can't take care of others unless you take care of yourself!

I used to love my body. I walked around naked all the time especially during my first pregnancy when my boobs were all huge and my skin was extra glowing.

Fast-forward two more kids, a combined 4 years of breastfeeding, crushing depression, jobs which kept me away from human interaction and I am just a hop-skip from wearing pajama jeans, a do-rag, and bunny slippers in public.

I mean, as I've mentioned, I only own the two pairs of jeans and the rainbow collection of pajamas. Where am I going in that? I do not have the tools to make myself attractive. I can't compete. I am a really, really mommish looking woman. I'm about as sexy as Nanny McPhee.

But the real roadblock is the post-baby body. I nursed three kids in 5 years. My tits have definitely seen better days. As the joke goes, my bra size is now "34 Long." Couple that with the tell-tale mom pooch, an extra thirty or forty pounds above my pre-marriage weight and a crooked C-section scar and I fear I must live a lifetime of self-love to crappy internet erotica.

I *did* have some post-divorce sex with a chef from Paraguay. He was a palette cleanser, if you will. He was very athletic and attentive in the way sexy, South American chefs should be. Our short affair was the perfect way to break the monotony, reminding myself that venturing away from convenient ex-sex is worth it.

Now, though, I am raising my kids full time. All the adults I know are women or gay men. I can't imagine a straight, single man wanting to jump on board with all of this - or even accommodate it.

Married friends say stuff like, "you're worth it, girl, he's out there." I don't think they know what the hell they are talking about. Reassurance from *married* women is not helpful.

I need a fairy Godmother to poof into my life, buy me clothes, do my face and then babysit. Otherwise, I fear that no matter how pithy my dating profiles are and no matter how cross-eyed, blindingly horny I am, it's celibacy whether I like it or not.

And since you're asking...

...the answer is "not".

General Life Update - June 2012

OK, for realsies, I don't know what took so long. I should have moved home ages ago. I am so generally happy that I just feel sad to think of the time I lost being unhappy in an unhappy environment, surrounded by unhappy people. Feeling good makes me realize, also, how few people I know back in Tampa who *are* happy. There *was* a lot of robotic, suburban defeat, though.

Not to say my life is not majorly vanilla suburbanism. I mean, I live in West Mobile with my three kids doing playdates and stuff. I am not any less poor. I actually have less time to myself now that it's summer break and we're homeschooling. But what's weird is that, in Tampa, I was always exasperated. I was living a little bit outside of my body, just doing what I was supposed to do. Now I am with my kids almost twenty four hours a day and I genuinely enjoy it. I enjoy *them*. I talk to them and listen to them. I hug them. I don't have to spend sixty percent of my mental and emotional bank on numbing the general malaise of a wasted life. I've got 100% of myself *to* myself. It's nice.

As for work and income, I've taken some odd independent jobs to make ends meet while I look for something more full-time. Also, with it being summer vacation, I need flexibility since the cost of childcare is astronomical. My ex still isn't paying child support.

How can that be!? You ask…

Here's what the uninitiated need to know about how child support works. The amount of child support awarded is based on income. Since my ex's business is mostly in cash, there is little income to report. I have no idea how much money he makes but I know it is next to nothing. Nothing from nothing is nothing.

Because of this, he is not in danger of losing his license or anything because he is paying what he can…nothing!

He *has* sent me money since we moved here. I think $200 in the last three months which is more than I got in the previous six.

I am homeschooling and the home school community I am involved with is boss. All the families are great, the kids have made a bunch of friends. I can't tell you how many teachers I have run into who have advised me to continue to home school, which is troubling to say the least. It's not for everybody, of course, but it works well for us.

I taught my 6 year old to read in a week or two. My oldest's personality has exploded, given the room to develop her sense of self on her own terms. I mean, she had a panic attack in Chuck E Cheese. Now she can talk to people of all ages - something I thought she would never be able to do. Ever.

When we pulled out a sheet and a globe and I explained gravity and the fabric of space she said I explained in 10 minutes what she could never understand in years of traditional schooling. The individualized attention is awesome. The activities and field trips are specific to what we are learning; what their passions are. They interact with kids of all ages instead of being boxed in with *only* other kids their own age. It's really been great for us.

I am not so rabid for homeschooling that I would never let them go back to traditional school if they asked. I ask them every now and then how they feel about it and they have no desire to right now. Things will probably change when they are a little older and I am prepared for that. If we keep up the pace we have been keeping, though, I don't think traditional school will be academically satisfying but we'll see. For me, home education is less of a movement or protest than simply an *option*. I don't know why it's so mind-boggling for people to imagine a world where we have options on how to educate our children, rather than some district lines and generations worth of poor schools in poor areas.

Of course, well-meaning and skeptical relatives try to "catch" me at failing at homeschooling by grilling my kids about their favorite thing they learned. I don't think my 6 year old is going to say "I learned how to read." So when someone says in a smarmy tone "So, what have you learned while homeschooling?' and she says "lots of different stuff" and they look at me like "mmhmm, as I suspected, no better than regular school" I just roll my eyes. The proof is in the pudding. The statistics about socialization and academics are both in homeschooling's corner. I am not concerned.

The only negative opinions I have gotten are from childless people with no background other than the extremist homeschoolers on reality television and a few educators who think I am somehow flipping them off by opting out. When I eat chocolate ice cream I'm not turning my nose up at vanilla, you know? It's no different with homeschooling, in my opinion. I know a bunch of amazing teachers and there are some great schools in every town.

As far as the kids' adjustment to moving, they are calmer and happier. We are all getting to know each other. Jaya and I are so close now. I think about how tense and unavailable I was to all my kids and now I feel like I have room to love on them. Kids learn quickly and have adapted to the new affectionate, happy mom. I think they like me.

I also noticed my kids have never, ever seen me pretty. I am still working on that one. That requires disposable income. But really, when I met the ex I was working at a "modeling agency" - quotations necessary- wearing heels and makeup every day to work. When I was pregnant I wore a lot of dresses. I was pretty at my wedding. But I've mostly been either depressed or trying really hard to go unnoticed during their awareness years, and they've gotten so used to seeing me in pajamas that they chastise me for even *owning* high heels like I've gone mad. Anyway, basic self-care is a habit I have to re-learn. The ex never had a problem with the fact that I did not get one professional haircut in the 11 years we were together, but *he* went on five yoga retreats. We just never had money for me and always had money for him. And being a stay at home mom I just didn't speak up because I didn't feel I had the "right" to the money. Drama.

The kids do really, really miss their dad every now and then. When he calls to talk to them, which is almost never, one usually ends up in tears. We had some serious issues since he did not call Jordis on her 6th birthday, nor did he send a gift or a card. After receiving angry texts from both of my parents he eventually called about a week later. His excuse was the typical tale :

I didn't know what to say. I feel like such a shitty dad. I think about you guys every day.

One of the hardest things about being divorced is that kids idolize their parents no matter how shitty they are.

It can feel a little alien being so involved in the home school community. Single-parent homeschoolers just don't really happen. So while the home school friends are great, I sort of needed a community who *got* it.

So I made one.

Upon moving home and reconnecting with old classmates and former coworkers, I was glad/disheartened to find so many of them in the same situation as myself. I decided we should form a group and meet once a month to cook a big meal together, let the kids play, and hopefully address each other's single-parent needs.

There's a mom of two I met in a "Crunchy Moms" group on Facebook. She's hyper-intellectual and her vocabulary is so big I often have to look up words after speaking to her. Then there is the mom of two I met at a family yoga event. I hinted at being a single mom and she approached me, noting how well-adjusted my kids are. We decided to meet a few days later and spent several hours on my bed commiserating, becoming instant friends. There is my former coworker who has one son. She works full-time to support her him and her extended family. One single mom of three was abandoned by her husband who went "on vacation," leaving her alone for over a year, only to come back with a girlfriend and ask for a divorce. My best friend from kindergarten is still in the process of getting divorced and raising her son alone. I remember seeing pictures of her magazine-glossy wedding on Facebook years ago and now it's over. And lastly there is a custodial single father who I was friends with in high school. He's a real-life Mr. Mom raising his sons alone, coaching the soccer team, organizing the carpools. And of course we include CBL, the Crazy Blonde Lady, our champion and knowledge bank.

Once a month we collect at someone's home, either mine or Mr. Mom's, and share food and stories of the struggle. Someone will pull out a notepad and say "what do you need?" and maybe someone will say "well, my kid has grown out of their shoes" or "the pantry is looking thin" or "I'm on the hunt for a toddler bed" and if the need can't be resolved within the group we get on our phones and reach out to our friends. Usually, the need is met within 24 hours.

Since my schedule is the most flexible, I am the go-to emergency childcare person. If money is tight or if a little one has the sniffles and can't go to daycare, they are welcome at my home. Payment can be anything: a loaf of bread, some bars of soap, some garbage bags. I don't keep a log because I know my needs will be met when and if I am in peril.

When my water was going to be turned off, another mama whose son I'd watched a few times paid it for me. When I was worried about groceries, my kindergarten friend, who is also an avid couponer, deposited a variety of stockpiled frozen meals into my freezer.

It's the best thing that's happened to me as an adult next to the birth of my children.

When I step outside myself and see how easily and swiftly a community can be built when someone just says "Hey, this is hard isn't it? How about we team up?" I am consumed with wonder, shock, pride and some survivor's guilt.

I feel like single parenting is easy now because having the community *makes* it easy. It makes me hurt for the single parents who don't have it. or don't know how to get it, or are too scared or prideful to ask for help. I hope I can find a way to extend it and include more people. It'd be even cooler if it became a "thing."

Like...

If I could find a way to create some sort of center or intentional community of single parents that runs on a barter system.

Come take a parenting class or volunteer in the daycare center and get to "shop" in our store full of donated clothes, toys, etc.

That'd be amazing.

Queen

I was treated to "bweffist" in bed today. Jordis made me cereal with no milk and a mug of water. I live the life of a queen.

The time has come – September 2012

Fair warning: this is a post about sex. Prudish friends and readers, proceed with caution.

Okay, seriously, I thought I was hormone-driven in high school. That didn't come anywhere *near* the cross-eyed, panting, blindingly scorching level of undersexed-ness I am experiencing now, two or so years into being single. But single-momming is so strange that sex, an act that used to be so easy and effortless, is now really terrifying and complex.

Why doesn't anyone warn us?

My single-parent co-op is comprised of women (and one man) of varying ages at different levels of single parenthood and we almost all agree on one thing:

As long as we have children to raise, we have *no* desire to ever share our homes with another man ever, ever, *ever*.

But we are humans. Humans have needs. One of those needs includes sex...but much more than that...

Oh, it's so complicated I feel like I'm typing and not saying anything. Lemmie try again...um...

The men I encounter seem to be in one of three camps.

1) They are married men who want to have sex with me, and are trying to convince me and their wives that we have threesomes.

No thanks, I've already been involved one complicated marriage and one is more than enough.

2) They are single men who think single moms just want detached sex and send me text photos of their penises.

No thanks, I've already been in one detached, I'm-just-having-sex-with-you-because-you're-here relationship. See again: Marriage.

3) There are single men who assume all single moms are looking to replace the male figure in their child's life, so they keep a half-petrified look in their eye the way introverts nearly poo their pants when the crappy magician starts scanning the crowd for a volunteer to be sawed in half.

Divorce rates for 2nd and 3rd marriages are abysmal. I need another husband like I need a kick in the shin.

So what DO we want?

I will try to explain.

I don't think there is a demographic less admired, desired or sought after than single moms. It certainly feels that way, at least. It feels like we are at the bottom of the heap. We are not available because we don't have sitters. We cancel dates because our kids throw up. Our tits are saggy because we breastfed thinking "no big deal, my husband supports me and loves me for me" never thinking that one day our saggy old tits will be up against those childless-woman tits that we envy.

We have scars and stretch marks. We clearly spent several months or years or, in my case, a decade in loveless marriages. No one was wooing us. We weren't worth the effort to our spouses. Some of us were treated like we were invisible, like slaves. Some of our spouses were cheating and drinking and drugging and making it *clear* that the threat of jail, or death, or genital warts was better than being at home with us.

So we left those relationships and now we are slaves. We have children with bottomless needs and jobs and bills. And we just want someone to notice us. And then screw us silly. And then get out of the way.

Single moms need wooing, and coaxing, and courting. We, more than ever, need tenderness and effort and finesse and confidence and prowess. And then we need a good, solid fuck.

I mean, seriously, we talk about this constantly.

We need to feel desirable again. We need someone to think we are beautiful and attractive and funny and sexy and smart because right now we live lives of thankless servitude. All anyone thinks of us now is "pick me up" or "I'm hungry" or "snuggle me." It's exhausting.

If host clubs were legal in the States, I'd be a regular patron. I would *absolutely* pay to be flirted with, doted on, flattered and sent on my way. It's 90% of what I need. The other 10% is not being satisfied through battery-powered means.

So in a perfect world, my single parent co-op and I (minus the man) would gather a collection of *single* men as it seems married men are all too enthusiastic to provide their services. These men would take us out on dates, love on us, screw us silly and never ask to meet our kids or stop by unannounced or get an attitude when we don't answer texts or phone calls (sorry, busy making home cooked meals for three demanding children) or want us to meet their friends or, God forbid, their mothers and *always* wear protection and not feel the need to show us off and be patient with our inability to dress properly for the occasion (we have little paint stain/vomit stain-free clothing) or the fact that we don't remember how to flirt because it's been years and years since anyone has flirted with us and don't mind our mushy mom bodies.

Something like a gigolo, who pays on dates but gets uncomplicated, no-nonsense sex.

Is that so much to ask?

Do Me

Being "low maintenance" has suddenly become the single biggest pain in my ass.

I had a rare night away from my kids a few nights ago. So rare, in fact, that I believe it's only happened three or four times in the last two or three years. It was always my mom who gave me the break, flying in from Mobile to Tampa to visit and help. Their father would only take 2 out of 3 kids at most.

As exhilarating as it should be to spend a few precious hours alone, it typically fills me with anxiety. I'm not anxious that my kids will be unsafe. I'm not anxious that *I* will be unsafe. I am anxious because one or more of my girlfriends will say "Girl, you finally got some time away. It's time for you to do YOU"…and I don't know what the hell that means.

The pressure of doing my alone time *right*, of using the time *properly*, is overwhelming and disheartening. As the countdown to Alone Time begins, I feel – no, I *know*– that I'm going to do it wrong. I'm not going to treat Alone Time with enough respect.

I've seen and known women who can stand and pound their chests and say "I'mma do ME!" with a kind of candor and confidence that I do not have.

I literally do not know *how*. I'm not trying to paint myself a martyr here. This isn't whining. It's my own tomboyish, one-of-the-guys, easygoing nature punching me directly in the face. It's my heroic flaw. I've never given weight to getting my hair and nails done. I haven't walked into a salon in well over seven years. When I feign girlie, I feel like I am not myself. Typically, I am left feeling inadequate and awkward. I have no disposable income. I am not going to shop, or see a movie, or grab a beer without feeling the financial impact of it for several days or even a week later. So what do I do?

Usually, I just lay around in the silence, or sleep, or clean. But no matter what I do, I feel like I am wasting that precious Alone Time.

Deep down, I know that laying in silence *is* me "doing me." But I also feel like Oprah is gonna burst through the door and make me sit down and she'll say "this is how you let yourself go" and I'll cry and cry because she would be right. It is eerily sneaky the way "low maintenance" becomes "no maintenance." Shaving your legs less becomes not. Skipping one night of deep conditioning becomes all.

I'm so utterly, completely over "doing" that I don't even *eat* during Alone Time because getting up and preparing food is too much "doing something." It's a damn shame, but I don't know how to change it. It's how I've always been! Before kids and the complete emotional mauling of divorce it was kind of refreshing to have alone time. I was skinny and ballsy. My low-key ways were considered "down to earth."

Now I'm a few years away from cat sweaters and mom jeans. It's almost *that* bad. I just never learned self-care. I can't help but feel like I'm failing at something. It's oppressive.

Palate Cleanser

Reminisce with me.

There is a type of sexual partner I think is beneficial to the newly divorced. I briefly mentioned my palate cleanser from Paraguay before but, really, the importance of this sort of thing cannot be overstated.

Let me sidebar for a second, though, and apologize for the highly sexual writing right now. It's as if there are unique stages of grief or stages of recovery or something and now I am in the "undersexed and horny-crazed stage."

It was really important to me not to allow myself to hop into another relationship until I was good and emotionally healed. I think I'm halfway there. I feel stronger, but still committed to just courting myself.

The sex part, however, is not so easily brushed aside. It seems to have affected all of us in my single parent co-op. Sex, or lack thereof, is all we talk about. But, for the newly divorced, it's all so complex. The last time I went on a date there was no such thing as Facebook or texting or Tweeting or sexting. There's a whole new realm of flirting and interacting that I don't know anything about and taking your clothes off with someone new is really scary...

...but that's *exactly* why you need to have sex with a "Palate Cleanser."

Let's start with the definition of "palate cleanser" for those who do not think about food as much as I do. When you go to a fancy restaurant you might be offered a palate cleanser between courses. This is supposed to cleanse the taste of the last course and ready you for the next.

In sex, and in our discussion now, it's that person you sleep with and want nothing more from than to help you forget your last relationship. My ex-husband actually started as a palate cleanser but I'm ridiculously fertile and was unbelievably irresponsible. I'm lucky all I got was pregnant, y'know?

But anyway, I'm a firm believer that everything is *everything*. As in, the way you perform your duties, the way you eat, how you regard sex and sleep and booze and relationships and *everything* is just a mirror for all the emotional gobbledy-goop that you're carrying around inside.

Typically, if you are a divorced person, you've experienced a few years worth of crappy sex because it's a common symptom of all the other junk happening in the relationship. Maybe the sex is mundane, or a little violent, or you've detached completely, or the lights always have to be off, or you won't go down on him.

All of it is a tiny version of the *big* problem. Your apathy, your resentment, your boredom, your insecurity, your hatred, your lack of respect is all evident in the way you have sex - or don't. So it's safe to assume that we, people-who-are-divorced, had some dysfunctional sex in those final months or years. That's why it is my recommendation that you sleep with someone new who has no desire to be a part of your life to help you remember how to actually enjoy sex again!

My palate cleanser was a chef from Paraguay. We worked together and I could tell he was interested in me. He got on the elevator with me just to talk, taking a 22-floor detour from his destination. I invited him to see a movie with me, just to see where things went.

And things went to my car in the parking lot.

It was that exciting, frenzied, frantic, desperately-panting sex that is so elusive once you are in a settled committed relationship – especially a failing, miserable one.

He was quiet and reserved but when he spoke he was very, very succinct. I was a divorced parent. He was a divorced parent. We both knew what was going on. We skipped all the fluff. Often, rather than wasting money on drinks and flirting and the dating ritual, we spent that same money on a hotel room a few blocks from the one where we worked.

And the sex was ah-mazing.

I was freer and more uninhibited with him than I ever was in my marriage. We did all kinds of stuff I would never have done with my ex-husband. And why?

The chef hadn't had an opportunity to completely lose my trust.

Sex is intimate. Sex is vulnerable. You're completely exposed.

And once someone has hacked away at you, emotionally, you are hesitant to give very much of yourself no matter how horny you are.

Not in every marriage, but in some, sex becomes a duty. It something you have to do to shut your partner up. Or it is a weapon. Or it is a manipulation strategy. There is little to no enjoyment left.

While I think it's noble and romantic to just be celibate until the next Mr. Right comes along, I think it's good to just find a willing, enthusiastic sex partner to help you erase all the sexual baggage you are probably carrying around with you. But only for a little while or your lonely, broken self will start to confuse things and get attached. No one deserves to be a human band-aid.

It's been seven months since Chef from Paraguay and six months since any other sexual contact. I feel like a crazy person and have developed a really dependent relationship on my battery-operated-boyfriend.

As one of my single friends said, this post-divorce, battery-dependent sex drought is like being a starving person eating Cheetos to get full. Sure, you won't *die,* but you're not even close to being satisfied, and day after day of a dull unfulfilled hunger is enough to drive you mad.

The fear is a little paralyzing though. And the lack of access. It was only when Chris and his boyfriend were in my house a few weeks ago that I realized I live in an almost all-female environment. Their male height and deep male voices were alien in my living room.

There are few men in my everyday life. Just one, actually. I mostly see women and babies. All the time. I know nothing of flirting and sexual tension. But I do know that sex can be honest and fulfilling and hilarious and athletic and adventurous and educational and tender and absolutely nothing like the tired sex of Broken Marriage that clouded the last 5 or 6 years of my existence.

I wonder what the sex equivalent of an amuse-bouche would be?

Cautiously pleased

So for a few weeks, my ex said he was going to plan a small beach trip so he could see the kids. To my surprise, it actually happened.

We drove to Destin and met him at a hotel. He'd rented two rooms. We spent the weekend swimming and boarding and eating.

I was nervous the kids would be angry or that he would be high-maintenance but none of that happened. We had a great weekend. It felt like we were co-parents. He didn't try to hold hands or get intimate like he usually does, but we definitely felt like teammates.

If it stays like this everything will be excellent. He definitely made up for not calling all those months.

He still definitely has not made up for not paying child support but...baby steps...

Adulthood – October 2012

This is short. It's just a random thought.

So, I'm thirty but people often think I am somewhere between nineteen and twenty-four.

I haven't decided if that's flattering or insulting yet.

But, at any rate, when am I supposed to feel like an adult?

I do adult things. I pay bills. I care for three children 24 hours a day. And I care for them well with, like, playdates, balanced meals, limited electronic entertainment and all that jazz.

But I still feel really small and insecure and young and goofy and unfit to wear heels and all that...

...just wondering when that is supposed to wear off.

Things Jordis Says

"I've been jumping around too much and my philophogus hurts. My ugulus does, too. And also my donbulus," so says the youngest child.

I think she goes to the Ron Burgundy School of Science and Medicine.

Stages of Loneliness

Being alone is hard.

Most people who get divorced aren't alone for long, gleefully flinging themselves into one anesthetizing tryst or soon-to-fail relationship after another.

But those of us who lean toward masochism choose to hunker down and run headfirst into "dealing with our issues." After evaluating with my single parent co-op I have decided that the ebbs, flows and pains of the "hunker down method" have clear and defined stages.

I present to you The Stages of Loneliness.

Let me start by saying that the stages of Loneliness and the stages of Grieving are not the same. I remember the "holy shit, I'm really going to get a divorce. Where's my Ben and Jerry's?" grief period well. And I believe, deeply, that experiencing all the Stages of Grief will help you get through a divorce with minimal thoughts of suicide and/or murder. But my personal experience and unscientific observation has led me to believe there are several distinct stages of Loneliness, the first of which being...

Nostalgia

Shortly after moving into my own apartment, and long before my divorce was even filed, I began reminiscing, fantasizing and torturing myself over every ex I let go and every crush I never pursued. Facebook became my worst enemy. I stalked like a madwoman. I pictured alternate storylines where I dated alternate men and had alternate babies or no babies at all. I blindly ignored all the reasons I broke up with these exes and never-pursued crushes. It's masochism at it's finest.

Torture yourself. Feel like an idiot. Feel ungrateful for the life and children you have. Deny all reason. That's the post divorce nostalgia.

It was around this time that I began sleeping next to a five-foot-long teddy bear I named "Joe" because it was a good default name. I'd never collected stuffed animals, not even when I was a child, but the vastness of my empty bed was unbearable (punny, no?) and I needed something to fill up all that space.

So here's my repentance. Sorry for stalking you Jason F, Joe B, Patrick H, Dan C, Jimmy H, Danny M, Clay G, Ryan H, John R, DD, Russ G, Trey C (I know, weird), Will J., Chad N., Jordan B. (two biggest middle school crushes - yup, went back that far) Rich W and Bill H.

My psycho nostalgia phase wouldn't have been complete without you.

A complete disregard for reality, statistics, experience, evidence and logic is what keeps the Nostalgia phase active and also helps with the next crucial stage of Loneliness:

The Rom-Com Stage

I have never been a romantic comedy girl. In 9th grade, *Natural Born Killers* was my favorite movie. I can still recite it. After that, indie character studies and documentaries became my go-to types. I refused to watch the Notebook. It took years and a handful of guys telling me "no for real, this one's good" for me to finally watch.

Yet during the Rom-Com stage, I devoured every Meg Ryan, Sandra Bullock, Julia Roberts, Katherine Heigl, Jennifer Lopez-starring nonsense I could get my hands on.

Falling in love in three days?

Yup, *totally* possible.

Last minute chases where hot guys steal mopeds or run through airports to boldly declare their love in sappy monologues in front of hushed onlookers so the heroine, taken completely by surprise, can swoon with dewy tear-filled eyes?

Sign. Me. Up.

I even found the unintentionally romantic movies exceptionally romantic.

Anyone else cry at the end of *Zack and Miri Make a Porno*?

Anyone?

No, just me in my Rom-Com Stage.

I still can't get through the first 15 minutes of *Up*. I have no idea what that movie is about. I started watching The Bachelor and The Bachelorette during this time.

But as I said before, one would have to suspend disbelief for a long time for the Rom-Com stage to last. Eventually, reality, statistics, evidence, experience and logic come crashing down in your lap and you realize that men don't typically run through airports to recite monologues to you. And you realize that every Rom-Com is about how the couple *meets,* but no Rom-Com dares show you what happens seven years later because you *know* what happens seven years later and it sucks and that's when the next stage hits.

Repulsion

I became repulsed - completely *repulsed* - by the idea of sharing my space, my life, my bed, my words, my ideas, my opinions with another man ever, ever, ever. Everything every man ever did annoyed the living shit out of me. I was *not* the girl to vent to.

If you said, "Ugh, my boyfriend is *always* leaving dishes in the sink," I would answer with "You know what? He doesn't have any respect and let me tell you something, it gets *worse*. First, it's dishes. Then the sorry motherfucker starts leaving his *socks* everywhere. Then the next thing you know you're married and he's telling you a woman's place is in the kitchen. Then he'll try to beat you and then you gotta run away. Dump his sorry ass now before it's too late!"

cricket, cricket, cricket

I frowned upon all your marriages despite my well-wishing. The statistics were constantly in my mind. Half of all first marriages and two-thirds of all second marriages fail. Why date? Why bother? What's the point? It won't work. It's just going to fail. I'll just raise my kids and then just be alone. Maybe I'll get a dog. But dogs die. Nah, alone is better.

But alone is *not* better and I couldn't completely hate men because of one nagging problem.

The Sex Brain Stage

In the last two months, I've watched the movie *300* at least twenty times and it ain't for the plot.

It's for Fassbender and Butler in loincloths growling and shirtless and sweaty for a full two hours.

Sex.

Is on the brain.

All the time.

I don't want to give away all my dirty thoughts, but I have a constant running list of exactly where and how I'd want to have sex with every man on my "hot guys" themed Pinterest board circulating in my mind as soon as my brain has an idle minute.

But, month after month of near-constant parenting and cleaning and disciplining and looking frumpy has led me to my current stage of loneliness

Paralysis

There is this strange dueling that goes on when you reach this stage of simultaneously feeling ready to date again, but also complete terror of even speaking to the opposite sex ever again.

Maybe that's a little melodramatic. My landlord is a dude and I can speak to him just fine.

No, but seriously, it's really scary. Especially if you take the time to do a bunch of emotional archeology and detect your flaws and examine them and change them or accept them. You start to feel like a big ball o'flaws. And you're so out of practice. And there are so many better options out there. Why would anyone choose you?

And then you have those well-meaning friends who say that their cousin's mother-in-law is married to a guy who married her even though she had seven kids and he treats her like a princess so I shouldn't give up.

And then you have those *other* well-meaning friends who say that the only men who would want to date woman with three kids are clearly either pedophiles or gay men trying to appease their conservative parents, so I'd better invest in a good vibrator and a Costco pack of AA batteries because it's the long dirt nap for my love life.

And then I think men my age who have never had kids or been married must be either a) perpetually frat-boying b) a reclusive gamer or c) not interested in having a wife and kids anyway. So I guess the pool is dry.

But this is where my unscientific study ends.

I do not know what is beyond Paralysis because I am, in fact, paralyzed.

I'd like to project that some sort of "Acceptance" is beyond this and I'll be one of those people who just don't care either way. Let's all meditate on that because I could use an extra dose of peace of mind.

Things Not to Say to Your Ex Wife

If you abandon your wife and kids by neglecting to take any financial or emotional responsibility, your parenting opinions no longer matter to the now single, exhausted, mother of said kids.

If your kids are acting like normal, butt-head kids, and your exhausted ex-wife puts them to bed and you hear one of them whining through the phone do *not* say: "Aw, they sound so unhappy. Was putting them to bed really necessary?" and instead say absolutely nothing.

You chose the life and existence you have now. You no longer have a vote.

Later that Night...

My 7 year old son, Jack, is singing "Goodbye Yellow Brick Road" to the girls to help them sleep. Happening now. Cuteness overload. I might vomit from the sweetness.

Blondie Claus

"What's something your kids want or need for Christmas?" CBL asked me over the phone.
"Uh, I dunno?"
"Well, like do they read a lot? Do they need some books? See 'cause my husband and I always like to do some Christmas for my mamas because we know things are tight and the babies need something under the tree."

Holy shit.
I don't know what kind of magical, magic karma is making this happen...

Thank You 2012 – December 2012

Despite feeling that humans, as a whole, have lost their humanity and despite my ex-husband being the absolute worst recently, 2012 has proved to be the best year of my life.

This time last year I was living a sullen, lonely life in a dark two-bedroom apartment in Tampa, Florida. I wrote about feeling punished around that time.

I read it now and I am glad to say that I don't even know that girl. It happened that quickly.

My moving home was exactly the right thing to do and in a creepy, law-of-attraction-like way by just making a few correct decisions, the Universe aligned me with the *right* people and the *right* circumstances and my life is so substantially different that my chest and heart swell. I can *feel* my heart swell, like when the Grinch's heart grew.

Oddly, though, the statistics of my life are actually slightly worse.

I have even less of a job than I had in Tampa. I spend even less time away from my kids. I've had two nights away from them so far since April. I get even less child support from my ex - close to nothing now.

But I have so much love that the technicalities simply don't burn the way they used to.

In Tampa, I was swinging on the trapeze with no net and no one to catch me. I was surrounded by people who communicated in contempt, condescension, bitterness, self-pity and self-absorption. With exception of Kelley, Bridget and my ex's one cool sister everything was black.

Since moving home I have crossed paths with some of the most fearless, uplifting, supportive women I have ever known. I learned more this year than I did in the 29 years before it - guaranteed.

Here's an overview:

The past is as relevant as you allow it to be - On my 31st birthday, I will have gone a full year without sex. As sad as it sounds, it is a huge accomplishment for me.

My life and identity were really separated into two parts: Before Marriage and Kids and After Marriage and Kids. I have not done anything else. Before marriage I was your textbook insecure girl using sex and male attention for validation. That insecurity is exactly what led me into the arms of my ex-husband.

He was a terrible boyfriend and an even worse husband but, to me, it was the punishment I *deserved* for being a careless slut. I was the ultimate slut-shamer but I only shamed myself. Even years of faithful servitude as a mother and wife couldn't cleanse me of my guilt. I felt like it was written all over me. That it was part of who I *was,* and that it would eventually creep back out and swallow me whole.

I actually felt *bad* for my cheating, drinking ex because it was *my* slutty ways that forced him into a life of domesticity in the first place. I *deserved* his anger, resentment, blame, and avoidance.

When I got divorced and moved to Mobile, my lack of childcare created a life of celibacy. I do not have the freedom for an active sex life. But the opportunity has presented itself a few times and I have declined. My best friend, Chris, even applauded me after I decided not to sleep with a former classmate:
"Jessica! You've grown standards!"

Yes, I have grown standards. I had none before, obviously. But this proved to me that my choices and actions are not "me." And those choices and actions are completely irrelevant now anyway. I'm not sure how it served me, subconsciously, to believe that I was unworthy of respect, love or effort but that twisted thought pattern is gone.

I'm worth the wait and the effort.

The only reason any of my past choices were affecting me was because I was allowing them to.

If someone shows you who they are, believe them.

I believe this is a Maya Angelou quote and it sure is the truth.

Things change. But one thing that has never changed is my ex-husband. Sure, he has more tattoos than when I met him and he drinks less, but he is still the person I met when we were 19 and 24, only now I can see him with my "reality" eyes.

I never had any reason to believe he could be a good father or partner. He's done such an excellent job of keeping everyone's expectations low that the tiniest showings of tenderness get blown out of proportion.

He spent two days in our house this month and, in the words of my oldest child, "it felt like a week." He has not paid even 1/5 of the minimum child support ordered despite being an able bodied, single, good looking white male who does not have to pay for childcare and has 24 free hours in the day.

I was hoping, by talking to him in person, I could understand why he is unable to take responsibility for the kids. Maybe there is an illness I don't know about, or some remorse, or maybe I can motivate him?

Nope. None of the above.

He showed up with no Christmas gifts. He contributed an entire $60 for the care of his three children this month. He wanted to discuss, seriously, his idea to move to New York to pursue dance at age thirty-five with no professional dance background. He ate my food and used my car and did not offer a penny for gas or groceries. He threw no less than three temper tantrums a day - raising his voice to me in front of my kids while staying in *my* house. He learned almost nothing about the kids. I watched as one of them would start telling him about their life and he would interrupt and word-vomit about chakras, yoga, stretching, essential oils, and the like. His son wrote him a letter begging him to grow up, get a real job and be a man. His response? Absolutely none.

Bottom line: This guy is a deadbeat. Period.

No amount of negotiating, discussion, threatening, begging, placating or ass-kissing will change it. And here's the kicker:

He's always been. I just didn't want to believe it.

In the two days he was in my home I felt like there was a vice on my chest. We had always been able to get along before, but that was when I was just *in* the shit. I didn't know there was another way to live.

This time I just couldn't stand to be around him. I swallowed my words so many times in 48 hours while he went off like a toddler because I didn't want my kids to think I was bullying their dad.

I don't want to influence their feelings.

I was so pissed I spent almost six hours at the movie theater just to be away.

It does not appear that my kids will have a good father. My ex is not meeting any of the requirements for being a parent. He is not here physically, emotionally or financially. My eyes are wide open now. With clarity and emotional detachment I can see that no amount of empathy or cooperation is going to change his behavior.

His family couldn't do it. I couldn't do it. His kids can't do it and there isn't a crunchy, bendy, granola yoga girl in the world who can do it. Only he can do it. And I hope for *his* sake he does it earlier rather than later. Kids grow up fast and he's missing all of it.

I will not allow him to affect my life. I will not use my mind or breath on him any longer. He showed me who he is. I believe him. I am taking action and I am done.

You really do measure a year in love

In evaluating this year to myself I tried to figure out exactly how to convey how much my life has changed.

Yes, I have moved into a house I never thought I could ever be in as a single mom with three kids. But so much more has changed, and it's intangible. What is it? *What* has changed?

Love.

I am drowning in it. It's everywhere.

Sure enough this Christmas, CBL came in the night and deposited toys and books into my garage for me to sneak under the tree "from Santa."

There was no way I was going to make those gifts from Santa. I wrote CBL and her husband's name on all of them. I wanted my kids to know how much the people around us loved us.

Love is all around us.

My mom, my sister, my grandma, my aunt, my uncle, my friends, my dad, my step-mom, my brothers, and you.

Reading my words, whether in this book or on the blog. You are invested in me, even if it's just to see if I've fallen off the edge yet or to judge my parenting or to hate me because you like to do that sort of thing. But, I'd like to think that most of you are cheering me on like the fantasy crowd at the end of *Big Fish*. I can feel that investment and it may not always be love but it's *something*. It's more anything than I ever got before.

It's December of 2012 and I gotta be honest I was hoping to be a light body by now, or dead from some Illuminati population-control tactic, or fighting zombies, or reunited with my alien family ('tis family lore that I creepily requested to be reunited with my *real* family on my "home planet" when I was about two) and none of that happened.

So if I'm *here,* I'm gonna be all over the place. I'm going to do everything I can. I couldn't have done it before because the healing hadn't happened. I still don't wear red lipstick. I didn't revolutionize the education system as was my brief goal upon moving home. I wanted to create an educational resource center as an alternative for all the kids who drop out of high school. It was to be a centrally located place, rich in resources and access to information. We'd do life skills classes, career shadowing, small classes and other sorts of amazing things. I got sidetracked by my own needs. I can't revolutionize all the things while I'm still unable to provide for myself, y'know?

I didn't learn how to play guitar, either. I didn't re-learn French.

But I did find myself – my *real* self. And I got the tiniest taste of what I'm made of. And I got to see myself through the eyes of people who actually care to *see* me.

And all of that is better than some silly old lipstick.

I will end with my friend, Ella's Facebook status. It is fitting.

"I resolve to live my life in such a way that future-me will be pleased with what I've done."

When I decided to leave my ex it was because I was ashamed of my life's work. I was ashamed of the impression I'd left on my friends and family. If I got hit by a bus, I didn't want my last days or years or months to have been steeped in resentment, hate, shame, guilt.

One year erased *all* of that.

One.

Year.

I may not have accomplished much on paper.

I have no degree to flaunt. My vocabulary is average. I have no idea what is happening in the world most of the time.

But there is so much love, and so much good in my small world that I *must* be doing something right.

Be a man – January 2013

My son is very skilled at articulating his pain.

The day after his father left town I found him crying to himself. When I asked him what was wrong he said to me, "Daddy's never going to act like a grown up and now how will I learn how to be a man?"

My throat closed. I have no idea.

I had always been sensitive to the messages sent by the media to young girls.

Despite little change in the sexualization of women and girls in advertising, people seem to be at least *aware* that it is a problem. Much more now than when I was little. Against the backdrop of the "Bad Girls Club"-loving America is, at the very least, a constant conversation about how the collective "we" is influencing a generation of young girls and perhaps confusing them about what it means to be a woman.

I come from a long line of independent women who can walk the fine line between lady and face-melting ninja assassin. I do not worry much about how my girls will know how to be women.

But strangely, as a single mom, I have become *more* acutely aware of the lack of positive *male* influences for my son. Or rather, the constant barrage of "life is too hard for the poor, stupid men" messages in commercials and television.

Last night, while watching some random prime time TV, I saw one commercial selling something. I can't remember what because I was so stricken with annoyance at the stereotypes. Mom leaves home to run errands and then comes home to the dad trying to change the baby's diaper on the kitchen island. The kitchen is destroyed because HA! Men are so stupid! They don't know *anything* about babies! Sigh, I guess moms know everything. Chuckle chuckle.

Jack immediately catches on.

"Oh yeah, I guess men are idiots who can't be dads," he spits out sarcastically.

The very next commercial features a man trying to show his wife the new juicer he bought. He was too stupid to buy a decent one so when the juicer made a mess all over the counter, he was also too stupid to know how to clean it up. Thank goodness women are born with the cleaning gene and know how to handle all the problems because all men are such giant dummy-head babies, right?

I am not simple-minded enough to think that the media is to be blamed for *all* the world's problems. However, I am perceptive enough to see that the "bumbling dad" trope, what was once a well-timed counter move to the "authoritative dad" of the 1950s, has become one of our culture's backfiring jokes. And since there are currently no men around for my son to see, I have to be especially vigilant in discussing these obnoxious ideas at length with my son *and* with my girls.

After all, this trope is a double-edged sword.

I am not comfortable with my daughters growing up and accepting that "lovable incompetence" is a typical male trait the way me and many of my peers did. And men, by capitalizing on this new societal norm don't realize they are only making their lives more complicated. What woman can *respect* a giant baby? What woman wants to sleep with a man she has to *parent*?

Then lo and behold, baby-man isn't feeling respected. Why is his wife *expecting* things from him? Doesn't she watch sitcoms? She's supposed to be hot. He's supposed to be fat and he shouldn't be expected to actually parent. Life is too hard. He quits.

I see it constantly.

Constantly.

On TV, in my life, in my friends' lives...

In a perfect world, I'd have lots of male friends who would pop in and visit with us, and my kids could build a perfect "composite" man in their minds to create a standard of behavior for them to model and understand.

But I don't have that.

And yes, yes, yes, I know there are plenty of good men "out there" but they are not *here* right now so it's really irrelevant.

So it stands.

I don't know how to show them what a strong man is because I can't find him anywhere. He's become as elusive as a chupacabra.

I like Adam Braverman on *Parenthood*. I think he's an excellent husband and father, but the subject matter on that show is so heavy that if I'm watching and they happen to watch with me I spend an hour discussing the complications of having a child with Asperger's, or having cancer, or being the parent of an adopted child or whatever.

I just worry.

I don't know how a boy becomes a man in a man-less world.

Dear Married Mom Whose Husband is Away on Business A Lot of the Time

You are NOT "practically a single mom."

If there is someone, resentful or not, who you can call or count on when the kids won't go to sleep, or your car is making a funny sound, or you need to kill that spider, or move the couch or hold your hand, you are not like a single mom.

If you can "run to the store"...ever...you are not like a single mom.

If there is someone who created your children with you, who calls you to see how you are doing, even if it's a chore, even if it's an obligation. If that someone who pays attention to you, at all, then you are not like a single mom.

If there is someone who you can bounce parenting ideas off of, right there in real time then you are not like a single mom.

If there is someone listening to you rattle off the details of your mundane selfless day, you are not like a single mom.

Listen, bad marriages are bad. Lonely marriages are lonely. But humans need companionship and despite how lonely and how bad your marriage is, it's not as lonely as *being* alone.

I remember, during marriage, when the day nearly took the air out of my lungs, and I was near tears and near collapse but I still knew there would be relief *eventually* because I had a husband.

Now I don't even allow myself the opportunity to *feel* the pressure because I already know there will be *no* relief.

There is no one to catch, or soothe, or react to my feelings. My feelings cannot exist.

And trust, the peace of mind and freedom and Self-ness of being single is a succulent luxury compared to the choking, stifling, emptiness of a loveless marriage. I am not minimizing that pain.

But when well-meaning women think they are going to find common ground with me by saying "my husband works offshore/travels on business so I'm practically a single mom" I want to sit them down, pat them on the head and say "no, honey...no."

If you can giggle about how you can't wait until your husband gets home so he can fix your AC/car/garbage disposal then you've already lost me.

My stuff breaks and I just...stand there...and know there is no option but to fix it.

And every time it happens I have a moment when I look around the room waiting for someone to walk in and help but there's no one there.

Yes, I learn, every day how strong and smart and capable I am.

Every time I have to paint a room, or diagnose a funky smell or sound from my crappy minivan, or take the panel off the back of my dryer so I can figure out why the heating element isn't getting hot, or assemble a three piece bedroom set on my own I am reminded how brilliant and strong I am.

But what about when I don't want to have to be?

Me Time

I know I'm supposed to have it.

I know.

I know.

I KNOW!
Again, I don't.know.what.it.means.

I don't need drunken nights out and can't afford them anyway.

I don't get my nails done. I don't get my hair done.

I don't want to walk around nonchalantly through a library or *shudder* the mall. That is not my idea of fun. I would be bored and itchy from idleness.

I have an amazing group of friends.

And they all volunteer and say "let me watch your kids so you can – "

So I can what?

SO I can WHAT!?!?!?

Go do...what?

What is there for me to do?

Comfort

Generally, I don't miss marriage but today I do because I really need to be comforted.

The last few days have been poo.

I'll elaborate when my head is clear and I'm not full of Pinot Noir and Pecan Sandies but trust that I went on a parenting roller coaster.

Today I got poo news about a childhood friend.

And poo news about a girlfriend.

And poo news about a new friend.

And I don't feel like I can hold it all.

And it's days like this that despite the "likes," and the well-wishing, and commenting, and "I'm here for yous," I just don't feel supported. I have no place to lay all of this down. There is no human there to nod or rub my back with concern and look at me while I ramble and say "mmhmm" or "aw, babe" or "I'm sorry to hear that" and it sucks.

I have been so enveloped in love. I have been so humbled and inspired by the powerful circle of friends I have cultivated.

But none of that is a substitute for arms around you, and a chest to lean on, and the ability to exhale and melt into someone, even if it's someone you hated the previous day.

Even when my marriage was on fire I still had someone to lean into when shit got shitty.

Now I want to get it out. I feel too full. But I look around and it's just the kids who need something from me and have little to give.

It's not their fault. They're children.

But children can't listen, support and console and shouldn't have to.

So I feel things, and just sit there hurting with nowhere to put it and no one to help share it.

The Mug

When I was in 7th grade I had a crush on a friend who was a huge fan of The Doors. In typical middle-school girl fashion, I immersed myself in all things Jim Morrison in an effort to deepen the friendship. In the end, the guy didn't like me back but I'd developed an interest in music beyond the Top 40 station.

The Doors became the symbol of my middle school experience.

But all of that had been erased until my mom found the mug.

When I was 20 and found out I was pregnant with my oldest, he and I moved in together in a feeble attempt to create a family.

He'd always been a subtly possessive boyfriend. None of the typical "tell me where you're going and who you'll be with" stalker-type stuff. My ex was fond of sabotage.

When I wanted to see a play with my girlfriends, he came along and drunkenly booed and whooped so much I had to apologize to my friends and we left. When my best friend had her graduation art showing, he promised to behave but got slurry drunk and made a scene. I apologized and left again. We temporarily broke up. But when he found out I went out with another man he drove across town to crash the date.

My social circle shrank until there was no one left but him and his family.

But he didn't just erase my friends, he erased *me*. I remember when he came to my apartment to help me pack so we could move in together. He took one look at my stack of yearbooks and said "We are not moving that shit."

"But those are my yearbooks. I went to the same school from first grade to graduation. Those are my memories."

"You don't need those memories. You said high school sucked for you. Plus, *you* don't have to move those heavy books because you're pregnant. *I'm* the one who's gonna have to move them and I'm saying they're pointless. How often do you sit down and look at a yearbook? Never. Exactly. We're not taking them."

And just like that, a chunk of my past was gone.

Next he took out my taste in music, mocking my love of boy bands until I was too embarrassed to listen. Then my sacred New Kids on the Block blanket.

I'd had that ratty blanket since I was 9 years old. It was well-loved. It was super comfortable but,more than that, it was a little bit of me. It was a goofy, adolescent, childish giddy me but it was me.

I was erased and I had no tastes or hobbies or interests outside of him for the next 8 or 9 years because I couldn't bear to have it ripped away again.

And I developed a compulsive habit. I became the exact opposite of a hoarder. If something wasn't useful, it was purged. I purged constantly and impulsively and cleanly. I went through 6 couches in as many years, just dumping them. They would feel like they were crowding me and I *hated* them because I didn't pick them so I would just get rid of them. I purged my belongings every 6 months. Compulsively. Then inevitably I would wonder where that awesome blender went, or why I no longer had that cute belt and then I'd remember that I'd tossed it because it wasn't proving it's usefulness that day.

I looked at everyone else like they were a bunch of materialistic pigs. When people had clutter in their cabinets or counters I felt bad for them. *I* only held things that were of use. I did not have room for sentimentality.

For that reason, I only have one picture of me pregnant and I was pregnant three times in five years. There are almost no pictures of my youngest child as a baby. Memories were frivolous.

I didn't notice this was a problem until his sister pointed it out. Still, I felt superior.

It wasn't until I had been out on my own for a while and, realizing that I owned almost nothing, I decided that keeping things around might serve handy at some point. Again, when I left my husband I left with my kids, my clothing and little else because there *was* nothing else. Just a few random boxes of books and esoteric knick-knacks that meant nothing to me.

So in my fevered, desperate desire to "find myself" after my divorce it became painfully clear that I was not reflected anywhere in my life. My life was hand-me-downs. Hand-me-downs that have *saved* us. But still, not very much of myself.

So now, a couple of years out of my relationship, I receive a call from my mom. We gab for a while about kids and nonsense and then she says to me, "Oh, I have to bring you your Jim Morrison coffee mug!"

"My what?"

"There is this Jim Morrison coffee mug of yours I've been holding onto until you were ready."

"Ready for a mug, mom?"

"Yeah, I wanted to wait until you got yourself back. Now you're back so you can have your mug."

So now I am sitting on a bed I picked out for myself, that wasn't handed down to me or from a dumpster. There's a pair of purple Converse on the floor to my left, a stack of books about reincarnation and astrophysics to my right and I'm drinking out of a Jim Morrison coffee mug - the last remnant of my "Self" from my life before my Big Lesson.

I don't listen to The Doors anymore but it doesn't matter. Jim is a totem of myself from when I was adolescent and *just* putting myself together, not unlike now. Jim Mug is just a lovely reminder that I am a *person* outside of my marriage and my kids. I existed before all of it, and will continue to exist when I'm done.

I'm still *in* here.

I'm still here.

Stages of Loneliness: New Stage Discovered – February 2013

When I wrote about The Stages of Loneliness several months ago, I was frozen in what I called "Paralysis" stage and was hoping and praying for some sort of "Acceptance" stage beyond that.

Well, I am happy to report that that stage, indeed, happens.

After the less-than-successful visit from my ex in December I decided that my hyper-vigilant, over-protective, paranoia-like fear and hesitation toward introducing any male energy into my sacred lady space was probably a little counter-productive. I started opening my home to dude friends.

It seemed to me that I was doing something good by limiting my kids' exposure to mentally unstable men but was skewing their perspective by not offering any healthy and normal alternatives. So we started socializing with my dude friends, like exposure therapy.

First, the "safe" ones - the ones who are happily married with kids and cool wives. None of them hit on me or abducted my kids so I could move on to the next step. Next, it was time to move on to the scariest kind of men...single ones.

That wasn't so bad either.

They were all very helpful and it felt good to let someone else do something for me. One friend helped me paint my daughter's room and even though I would have done a better job by myself it was nice to feel backed up. It was nice to feel like I was part of a little team. I forgot about those little "couple" things.

Anywho, the painting guy and a couple other guys started to catch feelings and I was willing to entertain it. I wasn't scared. So I started "dating" in the hopes of breaking my sex drought for my 31st birthday but guess what happened?

I learned that I have a very, *very* short tolerance for negativity. I don't like "Debbie Downer" guys who have a lot of negative, judgmental things to say. You know the type. They are so intellectual that they are constantly cynical and sarcastic? That is something I overlooked when I married my ex that I realize I can't stomach now.

I also learned that I have a very low tolerance for neediness and dependence. I am super focused on my kids and myself right now so calling me *every single day* is straight up unacceptable. Trying to guilt trip me into spending more time, when I am completely upfront about my lack of availability, is childish and annoying.

And (mom and dad, don't read) not, ahem...*reciprocating!*

NOT COOL.

I never spoke to or saw that guy again because no.

Ultimately, as one of my friends confirmed to me, I've gone this long without sex so what's another few months? I'm not giving it up for sub-par service or for lukewarm, neutral feelings toward the other party. No thank you.

So yeah "Acceptance" happens and growing standards happens.

You push through and suffer and cry through loneliness and you come out on the other end able to deal with and *be* with yourself. It's a bit like how labor and childbirth becomes the compass for pain for the rest of your life. I had two kids naturally and my anesthesia wore off during the cesarean of my third. So now when I, say, slice my hand or get a migraine I can always say "meh, I felt myself being sliced open. This is no big deal."

I can say that now about me.

Some random Joe who's "nice" and "has a good job" and "sober" but is negative, needy, and doesn't give a shit about whether or not I'm enjoying myself (y'know) doesn't deserve my attention or vagina just because he's *marginally* better than my ex.

"Better than my ex" isn't the same as "good for me."

Meh, I felt loneliness. I didn't run from it or try to put band-aids on it. Keep waiting for the right one? No big deal.

Oh yeah, that's something else I learned.

I *do* want companionship. It's pretty cool. I'm still not sold on the value of marriage for myself, personally, but yes I would like to share my life and time and bed with someone. Look at that turnaround!

In the meantime, I'll continue to date myself. If someone intriguing floats into my world, cool. If they float out, fine. I can't imagine that good sex would be enough for me to hang on to a relationship like it was before I'd allowed myself to steep in lonely and just figure myself out. Or, you know that absolutely-no-chemistry but he's "nice" so I-guess-I-should-just-date-him-for-not-being-an-asshole crap?

Been there. Done that.

Lonely is a choice. If you really work on loving yourself and surrounding yourself with people who love you for real lonely won't hurt.

Things Jack Says

"I'm going to be the President. All the women will vote for me, not because I'm handsome but because I will make sure women get paid the same much. And I will go back to '80s gas prices but not '80s clothes because that was just crazy."

Tension – March 2013

I don't remember what sexual tension feels like and it's starting to worry me.

About six years ago I was working at a place where there were a lot of flirty men in uniforms and suits all the time and I was very married. My life was sexual tension. It was everywhere every day. A flirt from this coworker. A wink from that business man. I had constant butterfly belly and my skin was always electrified. It was a good time. It made for a temporarily hot marriage.

Around this time I submitted two stories to an erotica website and got a good response. Both are still labeled "hot" which means they are rated above a 4.5 out of 5. Of course, I am hypercritical of my work and not really a fan of either piece but at the time I was proud. They were easy to write and I wrote dozens more for my own personal reflection or to email to friends.

Recently, I was talking to a friend who is attempting a polyamorous relationship with her husband and another man. The "another man" has ignited my friend immensely. When I talk to her I can hear sexual tension in her voice. I can hear that panting dizziness and the butterfly belly and electric skin. She says things and I can relate to her but only in my head. My body does not remember.

When a girlfriend tells me about the pain and mania of her spouse's infidelity I can *feel* it all over again. It lives in my throat and in my chest.

When I hear someone talk about their alcoholic husband/brother/mother/friend I can feel that, too. It burns in my cheeks and it makes me clench my fists.

But when my friend tells me about her rendezvous with her other man I can't *feel* anything. I can't remember the last man who gave me butterflies and trembly hands and tingly ears. I know it *happened*. But I've forgotten what it feels like.

I think about those of us who have gotten puffy as the years have crawled along. Sometimes I wonder if I've subconsciously decided that decadent food is the last real pleasure I have left.

There is little music or art – I do my best with what is available to me – but maybe that's not enough. The sex toys sure as hell aren't enough. And that's less pleasure and more necessity and mood control. There is no romance or touch or whispers or deep kisses but there *is* cheesecake. And it's velvety and supple and all there is left.

I'm sure it will come back. I still have a lot of work to do on myself. My self worth as an individual who can figure out and build and survive and create is strong. My belief that I am lovable and desirable and sexy is not.

So, I deleted all the dating accounts and I'm going back into the cave a bit. Clearly I have a lot more work to do.

A few days later...Owned

So Chris just owned me. Here's how it went down.

Me: I don't want to paint Jordis's room. I don't want to do anything really. I think I'm slightly depressed because nothing at all at *all* interests me. Nothing. I do nothing with any sort of enjoyment or interest. Not even cooking and you know I love to cook.

Chris: Now *that's* a problem. How do we get you out of this? What's going on?

Me: I'm just really glad for all the life lessons and shit of being single and really taking the time to work on myself, but I'm kind of over it. I want a partner (yes, already, after my "loneliness doesn't bother me" post). I'm sick of having to do everything and figure everything out on my own. I don't want *help*. I just want a companion, or something, to share some thoughts with in real time.

Chris: Are you still on dating sites?

Me: No

Chris: How long did you do that?

Me: I gave it like five months..

Chris: JESSICA! FUCKING NO! I'M GOING TO GET REALLY, REALLY MEAN, BUT WHAT THE FUCK EXCUSE DO YOU HAVE FOR NOT TRYING HARDER? SHUT THE FUCK UP! YOU GET ON EVERY FUCKING SITE AVAILABLE RIGHT NOW! THIS IS NOT A FUCKING JOKE!

Me: Lemmie explain! Lemmie explain!

Chris: You can, but I'm telling you right now it's gonna be some stupid excuse and I'm gonna tell you to shut the fuck up.

Me: Okay, well listen anyway. I look really gross right now. I feel fat. My hair has turned to cotton. Like, I don't have curly hair anymore. It's just Brillo pad or cotton mess. I have no clothes to go anywhere in anyway, so if someone asks me out it'd have to be somewhere where I can wear pajamas because that's about all I have and I look a fucking mess.

Chris: Still an excuse and I can empathize, but listen. You look a mess because YOU DON'T HAVE ANY REASON NOT TO. Getting your wardrobe together isn't a priority because you have nowhere to go. I know what it's like when you're broke and can't afford to go anywhere. I get it, but you NEED to spend at least $20 a week on some fucking clothes. When I broke up with Nate, I dated thirty men before I met Mike and then I dated fifteen or so more after that. Just to get out. Just to have a reason to wear pants because otherwise, you know our lazy asses ain't puttin' on no goddamn pants. I also miraculously lost a bunch of weight and my hair was looking good. You have to fake it. You have to get up, get dressed, put *makeup* on - I don't give a shit that you don't like it, you're 31. You need to just do it, and then you will have gone through so much trouble that you will *have* to find a reason to go out and be seen. You always said, "I'm not photogenic," but you never let anyone take a picture of you! How would you even know!? You're *shy* now. That's bullshit. You used to sing to strangers in Waffle House and ask random people you didn't know to the movies just to make a new friend. Fuck that. Seriously, shut the fuck up.

Me: Point officially taken.

Sistas without Mistas

I've been single parenting for about three years now. I have a lot of help. And even with all that help I'm still overwhelmed. But what I'm doing is nothing compared to what some of my homegirls are going through.

Here's the thing.

When a kid goes and shoots up a school, or robs a Circle K and it's time to examine the child's past and figure out why the tragedy happened, it's really easy to settle on and/or blame the "single parent household." And you and I know that usually (but not always) the single parent household is a "single *mom* household."

We hear that children of single parents are more likely to live below the poverty level, are more prone to suicide, teen pregnancy, violence, obesity, depression, yadda yadda.

After the Sandy Hook shooting, my Facebook feed was littered with generally bitter comments toward single moms. It's always the same old thing.

The women being blamed for "not keeping their legs together." Black single moms almost universally being assumed to be on public assistance while driving Escalades.
Yes, it happens, but not as much as you would like to believe.
Even during the Presidential election, when pressed for the possible reasons behind gun violence, a lack of moral code and single parent households were both potential reasons.

Even some women I love and respect are quick to jump on the "single moms eat up all the welfare and ruin 'murica" bandwagon.

No offense, but a lot of us single moms thought we'd be CEOs of our households until we died, crafting and fretting over cloth diapers and organic baby food. Sounds like heaven.

But instead we found ourselves alone and now we're just trudging through.

The math necessary for success is pretty unbelievable.

I think I could probably walk into a job making about $10/hr with my background in hospitality and rooms operation. So if I worked full time at a local hotel, I might bring home $400/week before taxes. The cost of before and after school care for three children – which I would need to work a day shift – is about $150 dollars per week on the *low* end. Factor in gas and food and rent and electricity...

I'll stop there.

If, like me, your ex-husband is not paying child support, you're even more royally screwed. People say "but there are systems in place to help you get child support!"

Yes BUT

In my case, my ex has no address (couch surfer), no employer (self) and no driver's license (he bikes) so it is not likely he will be "found" by the system anyway. Not for a very long time.

The waiting list to even *speak* to a person about child support was four to six months long. I am on the list, of course.

If you never thought you'd be on any government aid or support, the process can be daunting. The paperwork and wording is strange and if you fill something out wrong, there is a good chance your case worker will assume they've "caught you" in a lie and your aid will be suspended and you will be under investigation.

Because of the "welfare queen" stereotype, many case workers are jaded. They talk down to you. They assume the worst about you. They make you feel like shit for your situation. They lecture you on your life choices. There is no dignity in applying for government assistance.

Oh, and many times, once a single mom *gets* a job, her food stamps are instantly canceled or dramatically reduced. If there is no friend or loved one available to watch kids for free, that "income" simply goes to childcare and bills with little to nothing left over for sufficient groceries.

Some of my single mom sisters are ten to fifteen pounds smaller every time I see them. I know better than to ask what their diet regime is. I already know it's "poverty." They are going to sleep hungry so their babies are fed.

We had Year of Pancakes.

I misunderstood a question on some paperwork when applying for food assistance when I first left him. They canceled my assistance and I was under investigation. I had no one to watch my kids after school (not even one day a week – with several of the kids' family members within five minutes) so I could only work the hours my children were in school. I was blessed to have an employer flexible enough to allow me this. So I was working from 8:30 until about 2 pm, Monday through Friday only. After bills and gas and laundromat there was little leftover for food. Beans and rice and pancakes became our staples.

Pancakes taste like poverty. Still.

It *feels* like single parents have two options:

1) Bust your ass to earn enough money to keep a roof and pay bills *but* your kid grows up

parent-less because you are always working. You are forced to put your trust in "loved ones" and near-strangers and hope your child is never hurt or molested.

or

2) Be there for your kids... and starve.

We don't *want* our kids to be statistics. We don't *want* to be on government assistance. We don't *want* latch-key kids.

If we, as a society, don't want these troublesome kids-of-single-parents dumped into the populace all poor and bitter and dangerous then we *have* to support single parents. We *have* to set up systems of co-operative existence until single parents are thriving.

In my secret group on Facebook, single parents from across the U.S and Canada are taking the first steps to a co-operative single parent network.

We watch one another's kids for free. We send each other clothes when we can't afford any. We share eggs, or a frozen ham, or we buy extra band-aids. We pay each other's bills if the utilities are about to get cut. Boxes of hand-me-downs, cloth diapers, and baby slings are being shipped across the country from mama to mama. When a mama is in the weeds, we rally. If every mom puts a dollar in the hurting mama's Paypal account, then that mama can feed her babies, or get her car out of the shop, or buy a winter coat.

It's beautiful.

It's the **only** way we are going to *thrive*.

The only step beyond this is full, on-site support.

I have a grandiose vision:

I picture a piece of land. I picture small shared cottages or dormitory style housing. I picture multiple single parent families bunking up together and swapping child care and living off the land as much as possible. I picture outside volunteers doing workshops on self-sufficiency – car care, money management, discipline strategies. I picture free or reduced counseling for single parents and their children so we don't make the same mistakes again, and so we can heal the wounds inflicted on our children. I picture single parents staying on site long enough to finish that degree, or save that money, to be able to leave the property able to self-sustain and THRIVE with dignity.

I do not have the slightest idea how to turn my idea into a reality.

Here's what I do know:

I know there is a homeless mom with three kids frequently settled in her car in the Walmart parking lot nearby. The local homeless shelters are over capacity. We have, on several occasions, delivered toiletries and food to her and her family.

I know there is a woman very close to me who is suffering both mental and physical abuse and who *has* gone to local shelters for battered women but since her income wasn't sufficient enough to live off of after the time allotted by the shelter, she is stuck with the abuser until she finishes school and can get the hell out.

I know there is a woman living in government housing whose 14-year-old neighbor was shot and killed by a stray bullet. She is not safe in her surroundings, but she only earns enough money to pay $500 for rent. She has nowhere else to go.

I know countless more former wives and former stay-at-home moms trying to enter the workforce for the first time in five, ten, fifteen years – waiting tables, cleaning houses, and flipping burgers and sometimes having to *beg* their employers to let their toddlers come to work with them because they don't have family or money for a babysitter that day.

They don't need judgment, blame, condescension or pity. They need help. They need just a little time and a little breathing room.

I know that it is easier to raise a child than to repair an adult.

And I know that with enough brilliant minds we could do something amazing.

But my heart is too heavy not trying. I don't have land. I don't have financial backing. I don't have the slightest idea how one goes about creating a co-op on a large scale.

I *do* have a superpower, though.

I'm a conduit.

I can connect lovers and sharers and doers and idealists and together we've managed to save a dozen women and keep another few dozen afloat.

It's just that I have this funny problem of believing people can rise up and succeed and grow and thrive and be amazing after they've fallen.

Even me…

Milkshake

I just wanted to share a small view of the amazing men reaching out to me through dating sites. Please note that my profile specifically states that I am not looking for a hookup:

"Hello I am Joseph (Joe) and I look like a pirate, and yes avast ye matey I'll be boarding soon. How about a couple of porn movies, and you and me, and see if we can make each other happy? I love oral sex, and my beard would feel nice between your thighs instead of a rough unshaved face. But you know we might fall in love, only all we need to do is try. What do you say?
Seriously,
Joe "

"I am an older white male , and i like BLACK-FEMALES .. I have a private-place in Escatawpa Ms.... Nobody licks a clit better than me . I am 100% discreet . I want face , and body-pics .. If we meet , and you like me , how often can you visit me ?? Can you spend a night ??

"I like my women like I like my milkshakes, thick and chocolatey."

I am Jessica's utter lack of amusement.

Wolverine

Every now and then, my ex-husband calls to talk.
He doesn't ask to talk to the kids, unfortunately. He wants to talk to me.

He rambles about his "clients" and about what's going on in his life. I'm never completely sure why I answer. But last night's conversation was amusing.

"It's kinda hilarious how little women are interested in me. I think I reek of, like, pathetic. Like they can tell I'm a mess."

"I attract some gross ones myself," I answered. "I think I'm just gonna swear off."

He took a deep breath and then started.

"You remember that scene in that one X-men movie? Jean Grey had turned into Phoenix. She was just floating there and tearing up EVERYTHING with her powers. She was all glowy and badass and, just, hella powerful. That's you, chick. And I have this feeling that there is only one dude – someone like Wolverine with a metal skeleton – who can even, like, touch that shit. The rest of us just turn to dust."

"...Wolverine *killed* her," I said, "He got close to her and he stabbed her through her stomach, dude...with his claws."

"Yeah," he interjected, "...but out of *love!*"

The List

I feel like I have trudged through the septic sludge of my issues with men.

I can safely say I am no longer in that weird, terrified, I-am-too-damaged-I-will-mess-it-up phase.

I feel healed, rational, sensible – no longer like the addict in recovery cautiously avoiding temptation at any cost for fear of relapse. I'm okay now.

But being okay is not enough. I like growth. I like to push.

I'm addicted to the emotional violence of metamorphosis. It's kinda my "thing." So I said to myself:

OK, *Jess. You are comfortable being alone, sorta, but you miss companionship. You dated a little and you learned what you don't want. So what the hell do you want?*

CBL swears by a list, and for good reason.

Years and years ago, destroyed by heartbreak, she made a pact with herself. She made a list of ten or so "must haves" and several "extras." She dated each man for six weeks. If after six weeks the man did not meet nine out of ten requirements then the relationship was over. Completely over. If a man met nine out of ten requirements she would marry him. And guess what?

It worked.

She and her husband have been together for 20 years.

She admits, openly, that she was not in love with him when she married him. But they worked hard and despite recent major marital trials are still the happiest married-with-children couple I know. They love the hell out of each other. They complement each other. They accept each other. They push each other. They support each other. They're the real deal.

So, under her tutelage, I wrote a list of my own.

Actually, I mostly plagiarized it from another mama in my single mom co-op group, but whatevs, it was good. It's a start. And it's a much better start than the vapid list I wrote when I was seventeen that was all about dark hair, smelling good, and being hot while wearing glasses. Bless.

Basically, I used her starter list and then fleshed it out by thinking of the qualities of my best friends. I've had the same two best friends for 25 years. What qualities do *they* have that, despite fights, deaths, marriage, divorce, babies, addictions, and distance, we still love each other?

We still talk on the phone for two to three hours at a time, and it doesn't matter how long it's been since the last time – 24 hours or 24 months.

So here is my updated list in no particular order:

1. Self sufficient – living on their own, on their own dime.

2. Relatively intelligent – close to proper use of grammar, does not speak in "txt"

3. A bit of a minimalist - I'm a jungle woman, we all know this. I will always choose a cottage and a garden over a McMansion and a media room.

4. Orphaned or parents live in foreign country – This is not a deal breaker, but I cannot imagine having even more in-laws or getting enmeshed in another family.

5. Likes lots of sex

6. Is not allergic to cats – I have one. I'm no cat lady. I also like dogs, so pups are welcome.

7. Good sense of humor – I can't tolerate people who aren't funny. Isn't that sad? I feel like such a snob, but I really don't like to be around people who aren't funny. 'Tis what 'tis.

8. Likes to travel

9. Food adventurous – For me, willingness to accept and try foods from different cultures indicates a humility and lack of ethnocentricity that I find appealing. It means a person really, *really* understands that we are all just humans. We are all connected. What is good enough for someone in a small village in Ecuador is good enough for me. There is nothing "better" about our way of life and, by extension, us. And there is little more intimate than accepting food into your body openly and with trust.

10. Respects my boundaries with my kids - They are *my* kids. I have also written down goals and objectives for what kind of people I want them to be. I am open to suggestion, but I am not open to someone undermining me.

11. Positive, upbeat, jolly - Okay, look. There are people out there who are so proud of how sarcastic and cynical they are. I think those people are lame. I do not like these people, typically. I don't want any "Debbie Downer" types. I do not want to know why this or that is a bad idea, or about infectious diseases in the sea water when I want to go to the beach. In my experience, people like this can find millions of intellectual reasons *not* to do things and *not* to speak to people and *not* to go places – not my favorite.

12. Creative - He must write, sing, act, read, paint, cook, work with wood, dance around his living room, or appreciate any of the above. This shows me that "soul" health is as important as physical and mental.

13. Emotionally available, but not clingy - I will not play Wendy to another Peter Pan. Ever.

14. Financially secure

15. Responsible. Bills are paid on time. If said man has children, child support is being paid.

16. Dark hair – Just a current preference. I also really like gingers.

17. Upward curving ween - CBL said to be specific.

18. Sexually dominant - Again, specific. But really sort of important. I call the shots. I run the show. I manage a house. I dictate everything. I choose what we are eating, watching, reading, doing, all the time. I am tired of being the boss. I need relief. You get where I'm going with this? I think I can stop here...

19. One of my sister-friends pointed out that I probably need a man with his own goals and hobbies who "worships from afar." This is true. I don't really want to be enmeshed and blended with another person. I don't want to lose myself in a relationship. I require a lot of independence and freedom. I feel *more* loved when I have freedom. I don't want to be one of those couples who have no individual friends. I compartmentalize. That won't change.

20. Treats me like a lady. This is big. I don't want to be punched in the arm and turned into a dude-friend or roommate to have sex with. The ex and I had much more of a big sister/little brother relationship with lots of fart jokes and "dare me to eat that" and it was gross and exhausting.

21. Outgoing and friendly – I don't like to have to carry the conversation when I am out with a friend or date. I like people who can enter the party and go with the flow. I am not into someone needing me to constantly hold up their end of the socializing.

22 Peace-minded and socially liberal – Jesus is my homeboy. I am not legalistic. I am an ENTP – I will always question the efficacy, logic, and humanism of the rule book. What does the *most* good for the *most* people, regardless of "principle"? That's how I roll.

23. Treats people in service industry with respect - This is really telling, again, of whether or not someone truly believes they are part of the human fabric.

24. Values experience over trinkets. This is one thing my ex and I had in common and I was aware of how special it was. When people tell me how much their jewelry, purse, or shoes cost, I *instantly* think, "That could have been airfare to Hawaii" or "That would have been four tickets to a Broadway show." I just enthusiastically used a chunk of tax return dollars to take my kids to see Cirque du Soleil. I would never enthusiastically drop major dollars on an inanimate object. I *begrudgingly* do that.

25. I need something here because "25" is a nice number, but I can't think of anything.

So that's the list, but another friend of mine added an addendum. She has a list, too, but it is more of a list of questions to ask herself. I learned recently that no matter how "good" a man is, it doesn't make him necessarily good for *me*. So I need to remember to ask myself a few things even if Mr. Awesome meets 20/25 of these requirements:

Does he make me feel safe, physically and emotionally?
Am I attracted to him?
How do I feel when he's around? Calm, peaceful, energized? Take inventory.
Does he make me feel desirable?
Am I holding back around him? Why?

This is a start.

I don't know if I will be as disciplined as CBL with the rules. But I have never had standards before. Ever. I have also never dated someone I would actually be friends with. Ever.

So this is a start…

Me time Part 2 – May 2013

Y'all know I'm always a-frettin' over how I spend my "Me Time." Well, I finally cracked the case.

The only person who knows how I should spend my free time is ME!!!
I'm PMSing, y'all, so get ready to hear it. The filter is off.

The only reason I ever felt like I wasn't doing divorce and self-discovery correctly was when I allowed friends to *make* me feel like I wasn't doing it correctly. Every few weeks, well-meaning friends, who I *know* love me, start playing the same old tape.

"Just go out and do something by yourself."

"Just go sit in a coffeehouse."

"Just go take a class by yourself."

"You *need* time to yourself. Seriously. You *have* to have time to yourself."

Oh God, I must be doing something wrong. There must be something WRONG with me. I don't feel stressed out. I must be too far gone.

Eventually the "advice" got even more heated. Bossy. Bitchy, even.

"You are going to turn into a crazy cat lady."

"I guess you're just rolling over and accepting the end of your life, because you never do anything."

So I took it to Chris, my best homie 4 lyfe.

No one…

…let me stress this…

NO ONE knows me better than this guy.

So I asked him.

"Chris, my friends here are concerned I'm not taking care of myself or doing enough 'me time' - what do you think?"

Laughter. *That* was the answer. Surprised laughter.

The only person who knows what I need to "refresh" or "revive" myself is me…well, and Chris, actually, as he proclaimed that "with three kids, laying around and doing nothing IS you doing something for yourself."

No one else knows what I need to do with my time, least of all people who have known me less than a year or two – people who have ONLY known post-divorce Jessica.

I am not introverted, by nature. I do not feel "refreshed" by time alone. Walking around alone, or sitting in a coffee shop alone, or crafting alone does not sound like fun to me.

I've never been a "pretty" girl. I could give two shits about my nails. Getting my nails done does not sound like fun to me. And who the hell says it should?

Brainwashed women.

Women I love and respect. Women I know, and women I don't know, and women I don't like have tattooed the lip service onto their brains of what you're "supposed" to want and "supposed" to need.

Here's a short list:

When you get divorced you're "supposed" to get your "groove back." I assume this would be by sleeping with as many people as possible and becoming really fixated on the validation of male attention.

We are all "supposed" to need "me time" that includes vanity rituals such as getting one's nails done and/or shopping.

We are all "supposed" to need time alone wandering through the world with our own thoughts? I'm not sure. Again, I'm extroverted so alone time means dick to me.

We are all supposed to be exhausted by our own children and parenting. Spending the entire day with your kids should be difficult because GAAAWD, kids are JUST so ZANY!

I'm sorry I'm such a fucking enigma.

Trust me, it's not the first time a demographic I belong to is bothered by my inability to fit the mold. It was not fun being a ten-year-old black girl in Alabama who listened to Guns N Roses and Talking Heads.

So here's the deal:

When the people who have *seen* me and who know me and who make the fucking effort to know me start worrying, then I'll worry. Otherwise, please take your unsolicited advice on what I "should" be doing and eat it.

This, I promise, is spoken from a place of love because boundaries are love, right?

I am aware that people are concerned about my well-being because they love me and they care about me. For that, I am grateful and blessed. But, may I advise you to listen more or take this post as a cheat sheet:

I am energized and refreshed by *people*.

That is why, since I moved here, I have opened my home to friends and visitors at all hours. *That* is *my* "sitting alone in a park, getting my nails done." All of y'all who linger in my living room until two and three in the morning running your mouths *are* the "me time."

I'd like to go out and be more social but, again, I am *still* putting my life together. I have neither the wardrobe nor the disposable income for that sort of social life right now and, frankly, it's okay. I was plenty rowdy when I had the time and money. I am enjoying this time of sobriety and calm.

As for needing time away from my kids, please don't project your shit onto me. *I* like my kids. Sure, they get on my nerves like all humans do, but not as much as you'd like to believe. I *can* spend the entire day with them and be okay. I got it like that.

And when I *do* get annoyed with them, I have a big, amazing bathtub to soak in. My kids are finally old enough for me to do so without fear of someone putting their finger in a socket or starting a fire. An hour, bubbles, essential oils, and music is enough to refresh me, probably the way your French manicure does.

All of these things are things I wasn't allowed to do, for one reason or another, for the last decade. I have worked outside the home, on the opposite schedule as my kids, off-and-on since they were little. I love, love, love that I get that time back. My kids are finally old enough and self-sufficient enough for me to take time to myself. The bubble bath is a Bahamian vacation.

I'm fine.

I know doting and mothering is sort of the language of girlfriendship but listen:

I'm not the one.

When I ask for advice, I want it. When I don't, assume I don't want it.

My new friend, Jenn, said she was a "quick study." And she is.

In a few short months she learned that I really love bath products.

I am a sucker for some fizzy bath bombs. She deposits sugar scrubs on my kitchen island every now and then. It's a show of love we both recognize. And she acknowledges my innate rebellion against "the tape."

The what women/black people/moms-are-supposed-to-do tape that we've *all* been playing and believing doesn't – the fuck - apply to *me*.

So enjoy your glasses of wine, beautifully manicured nails, and long walks on the beach.

I'm taking care of myself the way I want to, the way that feels good to *me,* and I'm learning and re-learning constantly to let people's love in, and remind myself that their love comes in many forms, but to always trust *myself* first.

And also "letting someone love me" doesn't mean "appeasing their agenda over my own."

And on that note, time to draw my bubble bath...

The Book

True story.
My ex's parents had this really amazing history book.
This history book was often found forgotten in the bottom of a closet, but every time I found it, I sat and read it.

I'm confident that in ten years I'm the only person who ever did.
It was gigantic and had a huge timeline of major events, aligned by continent.
Eventually, the amazing history book found its way to their garage beneath a pile of other forgotten and unused items.

When I was packing to move back to Mobile, I told my ex's mom my intentions to either home school or develop an education enrichment center. I asked her for any unused educational materials she might have (she had LOTS) and she told me no. Despite piles and piles of unused Legos, dolls, toys, atlases and books she decided she'd rather keep them in her garage than let them be used by my children.

So I left, being reminded of my place on the family totem pole, being reassured that leaving was the best thing to do.

I left that amazing timeline history book behind.

Today a dear friend, whose children are nearly grown, donated piles and piles and piles of books and materials to me and mine.

Tucked in with the chemistry books, the literature, the math, the maps, and the magnets was – you guessed it – that amazing timeline history book.

It came to me anyway...

I'm not a religious person but every now and then I get a wink, a gift and a "you're doing alright, kid."

Rescue Mission

While scanning Freecycle I came across a desperate sounding post:

Hi! I am in search of baby items, furniture, anything! I have three kids and I just left my abusive boyfriend. I'm living in a trailer my mom had on her property but I don't have any stuff and I'm scared to go back to my old house. I need help.

Well, you know this didn't sit well with me so I sent her a message with my phone number. She called me back and told me her tale. I asked her the ages and genders of her children and what she needed. Her six-month-old was sleeping in her car carrier because she had no crib. I talked to her mom who said she was relieved to have the trailer available, but she didn't have enough money to furnish it. She lived in a small home with her other children and everyone struggled to fit. All of the clothes and toys were left behind. The guy was a loose cannon. I told her to give me 72 hours.

I got on Facebook and put out an emergency status:

Hey folks! I know a single mama. She's young. She has three small children. She ran away from her abusive boyfriend and she has absolutely nothing. For the next few days I will be taking clothing, toys, baby gear, food, and whatever else you can come up with. Share this status. Let's help this woman get on her feet. Help me help her, please and thanks.

Within minutes my inbox was flooded with messages. Within hours, people I knew, people I sorta knew back in high school, and people I didn't know at all were dropping off furniture and supplies to my house. Plates, baby toys, a crib, clothes, pots and pans, sheets, blankets all piling up in my garage ready to go to their new home.

I called her back to let her know I had supplies for her and she sobbed. Then her mom took the phone and she sobbed, too. I got their address and planned to bring her stuff at the end of the week.

I had to postpone, though, because then the gift cards came in. From around the country, thousands of dollars worth of gift cards arrived at my house from friends and strangers.

It was kind of fucking amazing.

I called to let her know I was waiting for all the money to come in so I could give her everything at once.

"You're an angel," she said with her thick Southern twang.

"I doubt that, but some ladies helped me when I was in the shit so I'm gonna help you."

In addition to the supplies I was able to deliver about $2000 in gift cards to her at her home. Sure enough, she was living in an out of a mostly-empty trailer.

But not anymore.

With our help she was able to live on her own and escape a dangerous life.

See, I'm a conduit.

I don't have anything but my big, fat mouth and more friends than enemies.

And with a network of amazing, generous people miracles can happen.

Male Stripper Syndrome

The common theme of the last week or so among my single mama friends and lady colleagues has been sexual liberation. But who is *really* coming out on top?

I'm a member of several single parent groups online.

While we probably should be complaining about our exes not paying child support, or the burden of doing everything on our own, or the shame we feel for being blamed for the demise of the nation, what we usually spend time griping about is our sex lives, or lack thereof. There seem to be three views here:

There are those still smackin' on the nasty aftertaste of fresh divorce who would rather be mauled by lions than even *think* about being in the room with a real, live naked man.

There are those who, after years of dedication to their children and soul-searching, are genuinely ready to step into the world of dating and sex with their dignity intact and their boundaries established.

I am somewhere between those two.

And lastly, there are the girls who got their groove back. They are serial dating and serial screwing to their heart's delight. They wave a flag of "empowerment," but from the outside appear more like starving people who have just been released from prison camps, scarfing and tasting every buffet from every restaurant that opens its doors to them.

Listen, I am not saying one cannot be sexually empowered, and I am certainly not slut-shaming. Everyone has an inner agenda, and everyone has lessons to learn from their paths. But it's easier to spot the ones that match yours. And there was a time, in my former life, when male attention was my *nourishment*. It was what fueled me. It dictated my personality. I didn't know who I was if I wasn't the prettiest, most intimidating, most man-eating girl in the room.

But my self-esteem was wobbly, and if I met a girl who was all of those things *confidently*, I would tuck my tail between my legs and shrink down to nothing. I was all coffee and no omelet, as they say.

Sexual empowerment is not the number of responses to your OKCupid profile, or the sheer volume of penis pics in your inbox, or the fact that you have a hot date every weekend. It's also standards, dignity, boundaries and self-control. When I think of the lies women believe about sexual empowerment, I instantly think of male strippers.

In my former life, before marriage and children, back when I was trying to convince myself I wanted to be in college, I knew a lot of strippers. Tampa is a stripper-heavy town, and broke college girls either take to the pole or befriend those who take to the pole to benefit from their soaring incomes.

I had a brief but interesting friendship with a male stripper named "Almond Delight." I don't understand his name either.

I'd met him on '80's night at da club. He was a good dancer and we formed a quick friendship. Inevitably, I was invited to see him dance nekkid. I dragged a girlfriend with me. We were thrilled. There was something really "girl-power" about the whole experience. There were hoards of women. My friend and I snagged a table near the front, our dollar bills neatly pre-folded and ready to be tucked into the banana hammock of the stripper we liked best. The feeling was, "Now it's *their* turn. Now *we're* in control."

I could not have been more wrong.

Let me sidebar for a second: I always love a good trip to a strip club. Men or women, I don't care. The bottom line is the camaraderie with my girlfriends and the stories to tell after. That said, going to see male strippers for the first time was slightly horrifying.

The first dancer was a stocky brute of man. After his entertaining slither down the stage he chose a "lucky lady" from the audience. He sat her down in a chair and proceeded to smack her in the face with his penis.

No joke.

And her friends cheered and whooped.

She giggled maniacally, half from enjoyment and half from the delirium of not knowing what the hell else to do.

The Brute then flipped her upside down and simulated oral sex on her while her pack of lion friends encouraged her to return the favor. She did, tentatively, and the crowd roared and hollered and the dollar bills rained down. This went on for another five or ten minutes.

Ragdoll "lucky lady", complete with beet red embarrassed cheeks, was tossed and pretzeled into various positions and dry humped on stage for everyone to see. Whose satisfaction is that for, one wonders? Who is really being objectified? Who is coming out on top?

I'm no prude, but I was terrified that he would pick me next.

It flooded my basement, sure. And I'd be happier than hell if the cast of *Magic Mike* dry humped me. *And* it was entertaining. But there was nothing *empowering* about it. I wasn't buying that old lie.

And while poor, uneasy ragdoll probably would have preferred *not* to be molested in a public arena, her wild friends - buying into the hype - egged her on. And so it is with the fallacy of "getting one's groove back."

Yes, it is absolutely possible to enjoy a healthy, physical relationship with no strings attached, but that's not what I *see*.

I see women doing what they *think* will make them feel more alive and more whole, but still defining their wholeness and happiness by the attention of men and the value they put on their bodies.

I'm seeing us accepting sub-par sex and not speaking up because we don't want to hurt men's egos. I'm seeing neglecting our jobs as mothers to pursue the wild side we never got out of our systems ten years ago when it wouldn't have looked like desperate insecurity.

Look, I am not coming from a place of piety, here. The only reason I "have it together" is because I don't have the option not to. I'm like an addict who just left rehab and is only sober because there was no liquor at the treatment center. Now I'm out and really only able to maintain sobriety because I simply don't leave the house.

I socialize with one man aside from Chris.

One.

And he is a member of my single parent co-op and we have no sexual tension. He is safe.

But I dated for a minute. Sex was readily available, but as soon as I realized I wasn't dealing with a partner interested in my pleasure and my experience, I shut the house down.

It's been hard getting to the point where my opinion of myself is the only one that matters. But it's been worth it.

And lonely single mamas, I've said it once and I'll say it again, take a moment and fucking *be* lonely. You deserve it. It won't kill you. There's a prize at the bottom.

What it *will* do, however, is force you to spend time with yourself and your thoughts and your feelings. You will have to start answering the "whys."

Why do I feel like I need male attention to feel whole? Why am I not enough on my own?

Date yourself.

And if you're going to the strip club, gimmie a call, I'll roll with you…

Today it Hurts

I can't remember the last time I cried, but I cried today because my youngest child turned seven yesterday, and her father didn't call.

I wasn't expecting a gift. I wasn't expecting a card. But phone calls are free, and she didn't get one.

He hasn't spoken to his children since January, but he has an outdated picture of them as his Facebook cover photo.

He hasn't spoken to them since *January*.

They don't even notice.

The kids don't even *notice* that he is missing.

They don't talk about him. They never mention him. He has disappeared.

And I am so angry my chest hurts.

I never thought he would be this bad.

I never thought he would be a deadbeat.

No child support, no letters, no phone calls, no visits but one to the beach for pictures with his kids. That is not love.

No one can tell me he loves his kids.

If you are his friend or relative and you believe that he does, you are delusional and you are an enabling asshole.

He uses his kids to give himself depth, to help him look human.

In his mind, they exist to serve him and to benefit him.

He does nothing.

He is nothing.

Most days, divorce is not so bad.

Some days it's paradise.

But today it hurts.

Robot

I'm a robot-alien hybrid.

I'm still really sad about my ex-husband not calling our daughter on her birthday, and it hurts in my chest. My chest is tight. And I'm so compartmentalized and emotionally static, generally, that actual feelings always feel new.

Tight chest, hard to breathe, general bad feeling all over body.
Can't identify. No vocabulary...

Emotional pain always takes me by surprise, like it's my first time in this body, or it's my first time on Earth or something.

Which is fitting, because when I was 23-months-old, I asked my mom if she was supposed to help me get back to my own planet.

Maybe baby Jessica knows something I don't.

Swallowed

Today is eating me. I am being swallowed.

I have obsessive-compulsive tendencies.

In my teens, I could spend several hours in my closet making sure the colors of my garments were evenly distributed and the hangers were evenly spaced. As a married woman, I could spend hours making sure the breakfast foods were on the correct shelf and the canned goods labels were facing out. When I got my life back, when I started regaining control, these tendencies faded. But today it's all back.

My throat is closing. My pulse is racing. I am fantasizing self-harm.

I want to numb it, so I want alcohol or a cheeseburger. I want to turn over tables and throw plates. Everywhere I turn is a massive, ugly, unfinished mess.

Many of these messes are unfinished because of money. The single parent bullshit in my face again.

Thirty bucks to finish this project. Fifty for that one.

Money I didn't have at the time that I naively thought would appear later. But it never does.

Someone always needs a pack of underwear, or we need laundry detergent, or gas in the car, or something. And the projects pile up.

And what was once a fifty dollar problem, when added to all the other fifty dollar problems, is now a thousand dollar problem. And they are everywhere, stifling my ability to function efficiently.

I cannot stand it.

And that's just the tasks I have to *look* at.

There are another dozen things I have to do. I have to sit down and shut them all up, and be on hold, and break up fights while I sit and get this shit done.

Right *now*, I wish they would vanish for a little while. They are so young and they don't know anything. They are not helpful. I have to stop to feed, to soothe, to break up a fight, to listen to a story.

If I could just turn them off for 24 hours...

I am drowning today.

In my head all I can hear is

help help help help help help help help help help.

I have to abandon yet another ravenous project to fix dinner.

Just *thinking* about it makes me want to fling this laptop across the fucking room.

The things people take for granted.

24 hours and $500 would *save* me right now...

Just 24 childless hours and $500.

Probably less...

I don't know what I'm supposed to do now.

I sort of want to bang my head against something until I knock myself out.
I also want to lock myself in my room and lock the kids outside so they don't talk to me.

I want to get in the car and leave them behind and just get lost.

Can't do any of those things.

So, with a lump in my chest I will make the fucking dinner.

I will leave the living room a mess.

I will lock myself in my room and pray they don't ask me for anything.

I will curse at my ex-husband in my mind for making me have to do everything on my own.

I will mentally flip the bird at the cost of after-school care making it nearly impossible for me to earn a sustainable living.

And tomorrow I will get up and do my best… again.

Because that's all I can do.

And it's pretty evident that my best is not even close to enough.

The Natural

Hear ye! Hear ye! I am here to publicly admit that I bought the red lipstick and still haven't worn it. I am also here to publicly announce that it doesn't matter anyway.

All my life, I've been a low-key girl. As far as beauty regimens go, I tried not to be socially offensive in either the body hair or aroma, but that was about as far as it went.

Not wearing makeup, as far as I know, has never been a hurdle or roadblock in my getting what I need, but I thought, up until a week ago, that I would somehow be left behind if I didn't hop on the train.

I'm 31 years old. At some point, I should put on a little rouge, right?

My naked face became even more of a problem when I thought, incorrectly, that I wanted to start dating again. Online dating sort of "happened" while I was busy in the marriage pit. Scrutinizing selfies and condensing the breadth of your personality into a couple of catchy paragraphs is hell.

I feel like I need a Public Relations degree to get through it.

And it made me feel inadequate. All of it.

I could never tell how much of it was just the "real me" and how much of it was me "letting myself go." I took it to my newest council member, Jenn, who slowly but steadily friendshipped her way into my heart. Jenn usually *listens* to me and *sees* me so I knew she'd give me sound advice.

And sure enough she did:

"Here's the litmus test: Do you feel more or less energized when you put makeup on?"

Less. Way less.

As a matter of fact, I feel like a fraud, or like a person in a chicken suit; it's *that* uncomfortable.

I let a friend drag me to the department store for a makeover once. She gave me blue eyeshadow and cherry-red porn-glossy lipstick. I posted a picture to Facebook as evidence of my wearing red lipstick, but I immediately washed it off because I don't know who that is. Objectively, she looked good, but she ain't me.

Naturally, I got a lot of Facebook catcalls from that picture. And that's… nice… I guess…

But I'm okay with not being known for being hot anymore. Me "feeling good about myself" means making my friends laugh, writing something smart, my kids telling me they are proud of me, my hair being more curly than fuzzy, wearing a cute dress. Putting on makeup does not make me feel good about myself. It is what it is. I'm not going to beat myself up over it. Sure, this probably rules out my chances of dating some hot beefcake, but I don't really care.

As Jenn The Wise also said, it's just not the time for me to stop what I'm doing and put myself on display. My heart and my passion are in rebuilding my Self. My head is down. I'm working out a plan. I have an agenda. And maybe the right one will see that.

And rather than me primping and posing for him, I'll look up, wipe my brow, and he'll be there: a stowaway who jumped on the train because he wanted to go where I'm going. He'll want to be part of my circus.

Or maybe he won't. And maybe I'll die loveless…

But either way, I don't think my fate will be determined by red lipstick.

Do-Over

I suddenly realized that I really have an itchy desire to travel the world.
I am fully aware of the fact that I now have three children.
But, I'm going to find a way to do it anyway. Maybe if I get a job that lets me travel and I can drag them with me.
I don't know.
It's a lofty dream right now.
But I applied to college. I'm going to go back and, just, start there.

Trust

It has been recently brought to my attention that not trusting someone who considers you a friend is apparently offensive.

I'm sorry, and it's nothing personal, but I don't trust anybody.

It's not that I have been burned or hurt so many times that I *no longer* trust. I just don't trust in the first place. I know that seems sad, but listen for a second.

I think people generally operate under the premise of "I will trust you until I have a reason not to." I'm the opposite. I need a reason *to* trust you. Otherwise you float in amiable neutrality. Not suspicion or contempt. Just neutrality. I don't think you're going to *rob* or *maim* me. I don't assume you're a *villain*. I just *also* don't assume you're a saint. But here's the meat n' potatoes, y'all.

There's nothing for me to trust you *with*. I don't have secrets.

Seriously.

I tell *you* exactly what I would tell my best friends, and the checkout girl at Winn-Dixie if she had time to listen. I don't keep any parts of my life tucked away.

I didn't realize this was abnormal until a friend and I recently had a long, hash-out-feelings, work-though-shit conversation and she said repeatedly that "most people don't know this about me" and I thought:

Oh, is that a thing? Keeping parts of yourself from people?

She and another close friend have both stated that they've been burned before.

This, oddly, is something I've never really experienced outside of my marriage. He is the only one who ever burned me, although, really, I think it's clear he only burned himself.

But I've never been hurt by a friend, really, or taken advantage of. Or perhaps I have been taken advantage of but didn't really care.

Not because I don't put myself out there but I think I'm detached from the outcome. I don't require much. You don't have to prove anything to me. If you make me feel good, you stay. If you don't, I just don't bother. No melodramatic banishments and tear-filled fights. Just apathy. Hopefully, this is making sense.

I was so relieved when talking to Jenn last night and she said:

"I don't really need you to trust me. I don't require that of you. My needing you to trust me would be more about *me* than you. You're fine. Do your thing."

Bless.

I guess this is unnerving to the general populace, though. It isn't the first time I've done human-ing "incorrectly."

But if you need me to entrust you with my darkest secrets and lean on you to feel like we're close, then I foresee a lot of disappointment in your future. There *are* no darkest secrets. Come over and sit on my couch – any of you – and you will get the full enchilada, if that's what you want. I've done those trust-building teamwork exercises without hesitation. I'll open it up and lay it out.

But here's the kicker...

...now I'm revealing a real nugget...

This openness, this quick warmth and close comfort is actually an extremely effective manipulation. My fellow Masters of Emotional Proximity are going to be angry that I am revealing our most potent strategy.

When we are so warm and so open and share so much and are so exposed, we have lulled you into a false sense of closeness, haven't we?

Please know that this isn't conscious. It's just what happens. It's my natural state. I can satisfy *both* our needs. *You* need intimate details to feel safe, to feel like we're bonded, to feel close. *I* need to give you whatever will satisfy you enough not to need more.

I keep my feels and my heart locked away because even *I* don't know what's going on in there. It's a mystery to even me. My heart is not really a "secret." Secrets, in my opinion, are *known* and then hidden and kept away from others. I *don't* know. I don't know what's going on in my heart or how to turn it on or what I'm supposed to do. I know it's possible, but I don't think it's necessary. I'm not in a stage where I can *handle* deeper.

I know all the open, bleeding hearts see this as a tragedy, but it's not everyone's life goal to feel all the feelings. At least not in this life cycle.

I treasure my friendships. I treasure their depth. I don't need to cry it out or have an after school special with my friends for them to prove their value, and I don't want them to require that of me. I just take what they have to give and am satisfied, and I'll give-a-plenty back.

And you can trust me, if you *want* to, but I don't care if you do or not, because it won't change my behavior. I'll still deliver the love to your door neatly wrapped and with a bow. But I will not leave behind a lock of my frickin' hair. You won't get an extra special piece of me.

If you're like the perceptive few who have risen to the top of the heap, just give me the space to be myself, drop all your Ya-Ya Sisterhood expectations and I will likely leave a few extra boxes of love on your doorstep while I'm making rounds as a "thank you".

What the What?

A woman I went to high school with, who I was not close with, and not friends with, just offered to pay for my kids to go to summer camp.

I...
What?

I'm not going to question it. My heart and feels are exploding with gratitude. I have no words...

Hashtag Blessed.
Hashtag SO Blessed.

"Friends"

Before you get your feelings hurt, allow me to explain why I'm about to unfriend you on Facebook.

I am in a fragile place. I feel as alien as ever. I do not understand humans, even though humans have been really great to me. Right now, with going back to school and trying to develop a non-profit and raising three kids and also homeschooling them, I really need the world to be safe, warm, welcoming, and aligned with my goals as a person. I don't have room for anything negative, or even amicably neutral.

I can't control the world, as it turns out, but I *can* control *my* world.

I've been preaching this whole "detachment" bullroar and I just realized I haven't completely been practicing it.

"I'll keep her as a friend just in case I need her one day" is people-hoarding.

I have to thin my friends list down based on nutritional value. Stick with me here, I promise it'll make sense.

Sometime a while back, I decided that casual sex had the "nutritional value" for *me* of, like, Taco Bell. There was a time when I could eat Taco Bell every day! It was so good, and the effects of it didn't really show because I was young and buoyant and didn't really know any better.

But now, I'd rather not *eat* than eat Taco Bell. It's just not satisfying for me, anymore. Even if I know it's tasty.

I think this goes for any and all relationships right now.

I'm in a place where I need all my relationships to be nutritionally dense. I am in transition. I need nutrients to grow. I need meat n' taters.

I discussed this with a friend and she put it well.

She reminded me of when Michelangelo sculpted "David." When asked how he was able to carve a perfect man out of a slab of stone he said he could see David inside and just chipped off the parts that weren't him. That's me right now. I am the sculptor and the stone.

In this part of my journey, I have to hunker down and chip away the parts that aren't completely aligned with me. The litmus in this process is this:
Does this person help me *grow*?
How does this person make me feel? The only acceptable answer is "good."

"Bad" and "neutral" are not acceptable answers right now.

Social networking has created a new bizarre and irrational set of rules for socializing. There is this weird ickiness associated with "unfriending" but maybe the word "friend" should have never been involved in the first place.

My *friends* call me on the phone. They stop by. They email me and I them.

The people who need me to be their comedian or their mini-Oprah are not necessarily my *friends*. They are cool and interesting people who I may run into or may not run into. They are people I like and respect. But that doesn't make them my friend.

And here's the crazy part. That's *okay*.

There don't have to be hurt feelings and drama. There can just be a calm acknowledgment and maintained mutual respect. Any time I have looked up and found myself "unfriended", I have thought, "Yeah, he's right…we're not really friends." I mean, it's totally cool to use Facebook as a networking tool or to keep in touch with your zany Aunt Linda. That's just not what *I* need it for.

I have very little adult socialization, so when I turn on my laptop to visit with my peeps, I need to it feel enriching and filling and hearty. I don't have "room" for the polite social niceties right now.

Yes, it's interesting that we went to the same school, or worked at the same place, or were best friends twenty years ago, or used to go bar hopping together, or I had a crush on you when we were in show choir together. But if we are not engaged in one another's lives, we are not friends. We are *spectators*. That's not the same thing.

Many months ago, my cell phone broke. I replaced it, but never told anyone my phone number. You know why?

Instant gratification creates entitlement. We feel entitled to portions of our friends' lives and time now. When someone texts me and I don't answer back in the mysteriously predetermined "correct" amount of time, that person starts going down a spiral.

"Where is she?"

"Is she mad at me?"

"Did I say something wrong?"

"GAWD TEXT ME BACK"

Um, who ever told you you had access to my time?
Maybe I'm driving. Or I'm taking a poo. Or I just don't want to. I don't *owe* you anything.

I thought that because I didn't have a phone I was free from this circus, but I realized it just carried over to Facebook instead.

When you share the majority of your pie and want to keep some to yourself, you're still going to have those people coming at you with a fork after they've gobbled their share.

That entitlement is such a part of the "language" of social networking that people don't see it as entitlement at all. If I go one day without updating my status, I get concerned messages and wall posts about my "quiet" or how I've gone "missing."

"Well, it's just that you usually..."

No. It's that you've gotten used to getting your "fix" every day and I had the audacity not to supply. It is much more about you than me. But you're right. I do spend a lot of time on Facebook.

So you know what I'm not doing?

Writing my book, reviewing paperwork, finding funding, reading my assignments.

Life. I'm not doing life.

So I'm thinning as a means of discipline, firstly. And because I just want people to water, feed, and sunshine me, secondly.

I will only be keeping the cheerleaders on Facebook. The ladies and men I have divorce-bonded with. The friends whose social and political views are different than mine, but who can discuss it respectfully, forcing me to evaluate my beliefs. The pushers, the helpers, the lovers, the believe-in-you-ers. And one or two people whose egos are so delicate that I still don't think they'd be able to handle my unfriending, even with this attempt at diplomacy.

Jaya and Changing the Future - June 2013

No amount of hovering and helicoptering can protect my children from emotional pain, but I'm starting to see that my parenting can protect them from suffering

This whole parenting biz....*sigh*...Okay, here's the thing.

One of my biggest fears when my oldest daughter was born was that she would follow in my footsteps.

I was sexualized early. I wasn't prepared for it. And it changed the next fifteen years of my life very negatively.

I was always a pretty child. I remember being four and five years old and people stopping my mom to tell her what a cute kid I was. But by the time I was ten years old, I was 5'5", wearing a bra, had my period for a year, and looked 14. But I was 10. I was a *child*.

But I didn't have a child's *body*. The world reacted differently. My first recollection of this was in fifth grade. The school I attended went from 1st to 12th grade. It was a common tradition for underclassmen to be assigned a senior who was sort of like a big brother or big sister. They would come to your class at assigned times and do crafts with you, or hang out on the playground. Typically, younger girls got big sisters and boys got big brothers, but due to an uneven ratio, I was assigned two big brothers, one who we'll call BJ.

BJ was an excellent big brother. Even though there were assigned times for him to visit, he visited on his off time too. He came to hear me recite my report on black widows. He clapped the loudest. He gave me a big box of candy for Valentine's Day. He remembered my birthday. None of the other big brothers or sisters did that. He ate with me at lunch. He pushed me on the swings at recess.

Only now do I realize he must have missed a lot of class to be so omnipresent. But he changed my view of myself forever. He was the first of many men to do so.

One day, I was on the playground with him and another older female student who was a mutual friend of ours. I can remember exactly where we were standing. It's a parking lot now.

He said with a dangerous-sounding giggle, "Jessica, did you know that when you are 18 I'll only be 25?"

The older girl shot him a look I didn't understand. I nodded and shrugged. Our ages had no significance to me.

Then he said, "So Jessica, would you say that you're...easy?"

At this point the older girl marched over and punched him hard in the chest. I still didn't understand. He laughed and ran away spewing false apologies. I didn't understand his words... but I understood his eyes and his tone, and I knew things had changed.

A few years later, I had a male teacher who I considered a mentor. We had a conversational banter, and he often let my circle of friends and me eat lunch in his room. My seat was the closest to the door. One day, another male teacher came to give him something. They were friends. The other teacher looked at me with *that* look. He muttered under his breath, "Is that the one you were talking about?" My teacher nodded. The other teacher let out a long, slow whistle and gave my teacher a face that read "Oh man..."

That time I understood, and it was tattooed into my brain. I resigned to the truth about myself:

Congratulations. They don't actually like you. They all just want to fuck you.

I spent the next several years pivoting on that central point. My oxygen became male sexual attention. My entire self-worth was steeped in it. This addiction led me to become pregnant my senior year of high school by a man who was ten years older than me. I was pregnant again a year and a half later by a man I'd known for six months. I married that man and suffered a miserable, high-drama marriage. Being a sex object altered my future. It's a massive chapter in my story.

So here I am, several years into parenting. My children are all quite pretty. When my oldest daughter was in 3rd grade, it started.

She went to a "good" charter school, in a "good" part of Tampa. She was close buddies with a classmate - a little boy.

One day she found out that he'd bragged to his buddies that she was his girlfriend. I've always been extremely open and honest with my children, volunteering information in ways my parenting peers would probably think is "too much, too soon." My parents spared me gory details and I learned a lot, lot, lot the hard way.

So in front of a few classmates my daughter told this boy, "Look, I like you as a friend, but we are not, by any means, boyfriend and girlfriend." His shame got the better of him and he went on the attack.

For the following weeks, he tormented my daughter. He flipped her uniform skirt when she walked by. He talked about her boobs. He drew dirty pictures of the two of them and passed them around. The entire class was enthralled in the drama. Finally, when it got to be more than she could handle, she came to me.

I. Was. Livid.

But more than livid, I was terrified.

It's already started. I didn't protect her from anything.

I asked her how she'd been handling it, and apparently she fought fire with fire. She'd told the teacher, but the teacher would only separate them and tell the kids to quiet down. I don't think she was aware of how bad it'd become.

"I'm really sorry, mom, but I called him a fuck-face."

"That's fine, honey. He *is* a fuck-face. But now I have to involve the principal, since your teacher isn't doing anything."

We went to the principal the next morning. My normally painfully shy daughter stood up straight and spoke with a clear and direct tone, and told the principal everything.

The principal invited the little fuck-face into the office, and for the next half hour brought in witnesses to confirm his lechery. He cried and whined, but eventually his parents were called and my daughter and I were dismissed.

I looked at my daughter, *aching* at the attack on her innocence, but I could see a little strut in her walk.

I realized I had changed the future.

Where I was clueless, she has knowledge. And with that knowledge, she has a voice. And with that voice, she stood up for herself. Something I never learned to do. Ever.

It happened again recently.

Now my daughter is 10 years old. She has her period. She is 5'4". She wears a bra. She looks 14. She is modest and insecure about her body because it is so different from her peers. She often walks with her arms folded across her chest.

I'd told her once about the episode of South Park where one character grows boobs and all the boys literally turn into cavemen.

"This is the truth, girl. It's real. It's what happens. You're a child, but your body is not a child's, and everyone treats you differently and it sucks."

"It does suck," she said somberly, but with eyes that said "thank you for understanding."

Anyway, my mom took my kids on a trip to a local water park.

While she swam, a group of young boys stood nearby whispering and pointing. In *her* words, "it was like being molested by eyes."

Finally, one by one, they approached and introduced themselves - clumsily and stupidly.

"Hi, I'm _____ and um, that guy over there thinks you're cute."
"Hey, that guy over there wants to know if you'll go out with him."
"Hey, I'm _____. Do you have a boyfriend?"

She answered directly.

"I'm 10 years old. I don't need a boyfriend."

This didn't stop the pre-pubescent hecklers who were now starting to turn on each other.

"You see that fat kid? Yeah he wets the bed, don't go out with him."

She answered, "Now you're turning on your friend, *real* attractive. Look, I'm just here to swim. Leave me the hell alone."

At this point, my son took up position near her as protection and my youngest daughter was splashing the guys directly in the face.

My mom stepped in and told them to go find some business, but it didn't stop them.

Only now, dejected, they huddled and whispered to each other but loud enough for her to hear.

"She's a bitch."
"She's probably a slut."

When I was her age, this would have *crushed* me. I would be an insecure pile of mess. Actually, it probably would never have even gotten to this point because I would have picked one to be my boyfriend. Because after all, the girl who hangs with the boys is the "cool" girl.

I would have been their pet or mascot.

But she has me as a mother and I am the *exact* mother she needs.

I can see the future. I can see around the corners. I warned her and trained her and coached her.

And she was ready.

When she came home and relayed this story, I was in shock.

It's happening.
It's already happening.

And I wanted to pity her and hold her, but I didn't because I looked at her eyes. Her eyes were eyes of triumph. Her body language was strong and tall. She was so proud of herself. She was so glad she stood up to them. I didn't want to project *my* issues onto her, but my issues are what saved her self-esteem that day.

We can worry about our children. But our past doesn't have to be their future. We are manipulators of time, if we choose to be. If we pay attention and if we are honest and if we get real with ourselves.

My parents divorced when I was young. My mom worked all the time to support us. I was a lamb for slaughter. I had no map. I had no armor. I was Red Riding Hood and the world was the wolf.

But despite following my biological footsteps almost exactly, it isn't the truth for her. She is Alice and the world is the Jabberwocky. And she is slayin' it.

Boobs

I am my boobs and my new bra is life.

A few months ago I got a proper bra fitting and invested in some new bras. I encouraged a lot of my friends to do the same.

My boobs, over time, have gotten unreasonably big. Or, if I'm being completely honest, unreasonably long. Three pregnancies in five years and something like five straight years of breastfeeding mean that I no longer wear that perky 34C of yesteryear. I'm lugging 36DDDs around.

Unreasonable.

If you have boobs I'd be willing to bet you are wearing the wrong sized bra now. A girlfriend of mine whose boobs have got to be twice the size of mine was arguing with me that it was impossible that my boobs are bigger because "she wears a 36C."

But just because you're wearing a 36C doesn't mean you're *supposed* to be wearing a 36C. And bra sizes are not constant. Your 25-year-old boobs and your 40-year-old boobs are not the same boobs. Come to terms with that.

Here's a short lesson:

If there is any puckering going on in your bra between your boobies, your bra is too small. You know that little space of fabric between your bra cups? It should be flush against your breastbone.

You should be able to easily fit your fingers under your straps. The support should come from the band around your ribcage, not the straps. If your straps are digging into your shoulder meat, you're wearing the wrong bra.

The part where you fasten your bra in the back, that whole strip of fabric should be under your shoulder blades.

Your boobs should sit comfortably between your elbows and armpits. If your boobs are aligned with your armpits, they're up too high. If they're sitting on your belly or sagging as low as your elbows, they're too low. Got it?

K, get your tape measure and get your tits together.

Anyhoo, before my recent chest investment, I'd been wearing the same two ratty, old bras for about seven years. The underwire was poking me in the chest, having worn through the fabric. I took the wires out and just wore the bra without them. It didn't support my boobs at all. But it did the basic job of holding my boobs in place and it kept me from embarrassing myself in cold weather.

The idea of dropping even thirty dollars on a bra, when I had a perfectly efficient one, seemed excessive and frivolous.

Let's really evaluate that for a second.

It was *too much trouble* to spend *thirty dollars* on something that would a) make me look better because my boobs would be in the proper place and b) take stress of my lower back which was creaking and groaning like a haunted house every day no matter how much yoga I did.

And thirty dollars for a decent bra is, like, nothing in real-life world.

But in the low self-worth world, apparently, it might as well have been a billion dollars. I just didn't care about myself enough. But now I'm single and kinda impressed with myself so dropping mad dollahs on a good boob-sling seems like a no-brainer. *Of course* I want to look better and relieve back pain! Doy!

But here's the funny thing that happened.

I got my new gigantic, expensive bras. I pulled them out of the plastic and tried them on and then guess what?

I didn't wear them.

I went back to my comfy, old, crappy ones. Talk about a metaphor for life!

The new bra, even though I *knew* it was better for me, felt restrictive and alien. The old, lazy piece-of-crap bra that was no better than wearing a few paper towels and duct tape, despite being less comfortable, was somehow *more* comfortable because it was what I was *used* to.

Oooooweeee, chile! Revelations are e'rrywhere. Ain't that just the way humans operate?

It didn't serve me. It didn't help me. It didn't make me look better. It made me slouch. It dug into me and chafed my flesh. It made my back hurt. But I'd already worn it for so long that it'd become "normal" to me. I had to consciously *choose* to wear the new bras. They literally force my posture to align properly - no biggole heavy boobs weighing me down.

And then what happened when I held myself up?

I got a little pep in m'step. I was forced to walk with some confidence with my chest puffed up like a rooster. And then I thought to myself:

Well, my underthings don't match my outerthings. I need some new cute clothes to strut in.

So I took a couple of bucks and, instead of doing something for the kids, I went shopping with my sister. For moms, this is usually very hard. It is definitely en vogue as an American parent to "always put the kids first." That's a theory and catchphrase that I think too many of us have internalized and taken to heart. It's as destructive as it is well-intended. What the hell good are we to our kids if we don't take care of ourselves? And if taking care of yourself is just painting your toenails then tell the kids to leave you alone for twenty minutes so you can paint your damn toenails. Or call me, I'll come over and paint your toenails.

(I won't watch your kids, though. Sorry.)

When the airplane is crashing, you put the oxygen mask on yourself and *then* on your child. Why? Because your child is helpless without you; you have to take care of yourself.

It was hard shopping for myself at first. I literally hadn't done it in years and years. When the seasons changed, it always caught me off guard and I'd end up wearing some friend's hand-me-downs to "get through." I never looked like myself on the outside. But at least I wasn't nekkid. That was the best I wanted for myself - just the bare minimum.

Just "not nekkid."

So I got a few cute dresses that looked like "me." And I wear them with some cute bracelets and cute shoes. And then sometimes, because I have a cute outfit on, I have to put some face on. And then, without red lipstick, I became the kind of person who will not leave the house in yoga pants.

Not that there's anything wrong with that. If "I just want to be comfortable" is your goal, then by all means. But that, *for me*, was an excuse. I now refer to them as "gave up pants" because that's what they were when I was wearing them.

I know some of you "just got done working out" so you walk around in your workout clothes, but this is something that is very American. In many countries, workout clothes are for working out and they are left at that. They don't double as *clothes*. They're like pajamas or lingerie. Just a little fun fact.

But it is shocking to me how, when you really start to care about yourself and make yourself a priority, it does not feel like extra work to put on a cute dress. It feels as natural as waking up and brushing your teeth. And it's born from self-love!

It's crazy!

I'm not dressing cute so guys will think I'm hot or so I'm the foxiest mom at the playground. I don't care about the guys or the other moms! I actually, *finally*, and really for real truly look cute for *me!* Like, for real.

Self-love is REAL.

And all because of my sorry, saggy boobs!
And check this out. You can want to improve yourself while *simultaneously* loving yourself.

Could you imagine such a thing?

You don't have to *hate* your boobs or your thighs or your self to want to change them. It's just bananas.

I got a little ways to go, still.

I'm still much chubbier than I'd like to get comfortable with, but holy shit I *never* thought I'd be the kind of person who actually got dressed. I thought my schlumpy perma-pajama thing was part of my charm. It was part of my quirk. But I know now that the schlumpy clothes and schlumpy boobs were really just a symptom of low self-worth.

BOOM!

Educated by my tits, y'all.

I decided to take my new revelations to my friends and slowly they started to join "the movement." Some called it the "Get Dressed Challenge." For so many stay at home moms and home school moms it's easier not to. But then it becomes cyclical and going and doing things feels difficult because, *sigh*, you'd have to put on *pants*. But there is something really busy-making and feel-goodish about waking up and hoisting your boobs up and putting on "hard pants" at the top of your day. You just feel capable.

So my lady friends started posting pics of themselves dressed every day, in hard pants and with makeup on their faces. We cheered each other on. It was pretty groovy. And all this goodness coming from a bra dilemma!

Old. Alone. Done For.

I've been thinking about my eventual death a lot lately.
It's not my mortality, necessarily, that scares me.

Aside from zombies, the only thing I am really afraid of is dying unloved.

Before you start crying rivers, please know I do not want pity or sad face emoticons. But if you feel sad for me, then by all means. Death is not something that makes *me* feel sad or scared. Typically, when I lose someone close to me, or someone young I am more humbly shocked than anything. I have a robotic "healthy" relationship with death as a reality, I think. I know I will lose everyone one day and they will lose me. I know I could run out to the store for milk and not come back. It is "morbid" to many but I'm a Pisces and my parents let me watch Beetlejuice when I was five so morbid is familiar and comfortable territory for me.

Even though I am only thirty-one, I am touched by only one degree by shortened lives or at least potentially shortened ones. Friends my age are being diagnosed with or dying from cancer. I never had that infinite feeling that goes along with being young and daffy. My mortality is what prompted me to file for divorce and leave my ex-husband. The day with the garbage can was the changing day. I realized then that if I died that day in the driveway covered in maggots I'd done absolutely nothing to feel proud of. My legacy and the last memories my loved ones would have would be of me fat, depressed, angry and unaccomplished. I am only a few short years beyond that day and *so* much has changed.

I am thirsty to finish my education with a ferocious clarity I have never before experienced. I am homeschooling my kids and they are *thriving* - academically and socially. I am molding them to become *exactly* who I'd hoped they'd be: questioning, challenging, open-minded, worldly, and courteous.

Through the common journey of single-parenthood I have made so many close friends from around the country - other lady warriors not content to just keep their own raft afloat but to share a bail bucket with their sisters in need.

I've taken the last few years to so some seeeeeerious emotional work. I've cleansed myself of the demons that haunted the first twenty-five years of my life, determined not to take them into my future - or worse - allow them to taint future generations. I am, however, still pretty fat.

Shrug

But all in all, if I go out for milk and get struck by a car, or mugged and shot, or a triceratops stampede comes and runs me over, my little soul will float away feeling 80% okay about my life. I think that, for being thirty-one, that ain't bad. I try really hard to feel grateful for at least that.

However, the nagging itchy 20% is dissatisfaction belonging to *one* truth. I've never been in love with anyone and no one's ever been in love with me.

Oh, but you still have time...

Well, it's time that is not exactly guaranteed or owed to me.

You know your twenties, when you're dating and falling in love and focusing on yourself and all that? I didn't do that. My ex and I moved in together when I was 19, after knowing each other for 6 months and after finding out I was pregnant. I was not in love with him. He was not in love with me. But by some bizarre "code of honor," that in the end he did not actually believe in, he insisted we stay together for the sake of the baby. And I, embarrassed and determined not to go home to my family a knocked-up failure, agreed.

I always knew he was not a good partner but my fear of being alone, and my fear of being "a single black welfare mom," was bigger than my desire to self-preserve.

We, eventually, loved each other in some sort of way, I guess. But we loved each other the way two castaways on a deserted island grow to eventually love each other. You just try to *not die* together and there's no one else to talk to - so you eventually sort of love each other. It's more like Stockholm syndrome, really. I was isolated and have no perspective.

So now I'm single and I have three kids and I worry that I will never find love.

It's not because I don't think I'm worthy. I know I am.

I'm whip-smart. I'm hilarious. I'm empathetic. I'm a good-listener. I'm open-minded. Very little is taboo to me. I got it going on.

I'm too busy making myself exceptionally awesome to have time to date.

I am focused on getting myself so "on top of it" that I will never, ever, ever, ever find myself in a two bedroom apartment with three kids and one mattress eating rice and beans every night because we're poor ever again.

EVER.

But, no, my fear of dying unloved really comes from time.

I'm going to be in school for the next 3 years *minimum*. Then I'll be out in the world working and will maybe be in a place, emotionally, to begin dating. Anything can happen and I don't know if I'll be able to squeeze it in before I take the long dirt nap. But, as a person who thrives in a chaotic environment, the fact that I'm actually planning and taking steps really fills me with a mild sort of dread.

Right now I'm "doing it right."

I'm not dating before I'm ready. I'm going back to school. I'm focused on the mental health of myself and my kids. I'm not allowing myself to be led by my vagina or my loneliness or insecurity.

I see my fellow single mom sistahs get pulled in, left and right, into these short-lived flings and I feel for them but I am so glad I am not in their place.

One single lady in particular is so blinded by her fear of being alone that I am puh-retty sure her boyfriend is a predator. He grooms and gives me the mad creeps. But no amount of warning can sway her. She is positive he's a gentleman despite there being no consistent evidence for that to be true.

I'm not in that place, emotionally. I've got a rational, logical, data-backed plan.

But what if I don't get the cheese at the end?

And in five or ten years, with my degree and my healthy kids I shout "ok world, I'm ready for love" and then BAM! Zombie apocalypse and I'm dead. No love for Jess.

I exaggerate of course, but really, planning is scary because you are taking yourself out of the present, *on purpose*, to create a reality that will hopefully come sometime down-the-line with no guarantee that it *will*.

That kind of love is not *owed* to me. I do not *deserve* it. None of us do. It's just a gift if we can get it. It's like a good parking space or a crab leg that cracks perfectly and you can get that big, whole piece of crab, y'know what I'm talking about? It's amazing when it happens but it's not, like, a guarantee or even a right. It's a sweet, precious, surprise, luxury, happy event.

Millions of people die every day without having ever been in love. People die without ever seeing their children grow up. I noticed that when someone young passes away, it is often customary for people to say "they were taken before their time." But who ever said we were owed all this time in the first place? What do we know about how much time people are supposed to have? Humans are fragile and can die at any time.

That seems to be a conflict of perspective.

I am gravely aware that neither time nor romantic love is owed to me.

And that realization kinda bums me out.

So even though I hope to maybe one day meet the man I'm supposed to be with I still have to sit in, and accept, the *possibility* that it won't happen.

And the love of my kids and the platonic love of my friends might be the only love I get this time around. And that is a little scary and also a little sad.

And every "it'll happen" just boils my blood.

I was telling Jenn on the phone, "I never had time to be in love. I was nineteen when I got pregnant and twenty-nine when I left him. My entire adulthood up until now has been orbiting around him. I know I'm worthy of love, yes. But I do not believe there are many men out there willing to sign on to a woman with three kids who can't have any more. I mean I could be one of those women who gets pregnant despite having her tubes tied, but still. Even if he did exist, I do not want to blend families. I think it significantly increases the risk of divorce and I'm still tied to my ex's family. I don't want any more in-laws if I can help it as that would give my kids something like five or six sets of grandparents. The pool of available men gets smaller and smaller and smaller, and I know *so clearly* what I want and need and that makes the pool even *smaller* and *if* he is out there, will I even meet him and. even worse, what if he doesn't even exist?"

And after interrogating and pushing and questioning and offering advice and insight when she finally *got it* all she could say was "damn, that sucks."

And yeah, that's all there is to say.

I'm kind of a robot. I'm really rational. It's possibly my best quality since, according to her, even though I cannot join people in grieving and crying and I have no real emotional highs and lows of my own, it is for that reason that I am a good go-to woman for making people feel stable, for offering facts and data. I'm a true ENTP.

But, because of my brain-first approach to everything I worry I won't "turn on" my feelings in time. It's crazy.

It's a shit realization that totally sucks and there's nothing more to it.

It's a fleeting feeling, like all my feelings, that sneaks in late at night and gnaws at my earlobes until I give it a little attention. Usually, it's gone by morning.

I'm not walking around paranoid or worried about some Final Destination-esque freak accident. But I'm also not presumptuous enough to think I've got all the time in the world to develop myself as a person *and* find Prince Charming.

It's one of those times I wish I was the kind of person who thought little beyond what pants to wear and feeding the dog and football season.

Love is the only box left to check and I don't wanna go with it empty.

Everything He Needs

Earlier this year I was beside myself trying to figure out how to find positive male role models for my son. He'd grown prone to apologizing before or after speaking. He was passive. This worried me.

We went to counseling for a while but, with our poor-people insurance, ended up with an apathetic counselor. He really just reinforced Jack's middle-child-syndrome by barely listening and zoning out while he was talking.

A male friend of mine came over a few times to watch movies and play but eventually got back into his single-person life and hasn't been over in months. I was so worried Jack would feel re-abandoned.

We were sitting outside one day and Jack was playing with some sticks in the front yard, trying to fashion himself a bow and arrow. The girls were making bows and arrows, too. I called out to him, "Maybe your Uncle Terry can come over and hang out with you, Jack, and you guys can make arrows together."

He nodded apathetically and then I was stricken with some wisdom.

It's my fault.

It's *all* my fault.

He wasn't meek and passive because he didn't have a male role model. He's meek and passive because I didn't even give him a chance to feel okay. I *told* him his life was lacking without a man in it. *I* put that hole there.

This is hard to explain but bear with me.

The story is that little boys need a male role model so they know how to be a man. So single-moms need to busy themselves with finding a man for their sons to look up to.

But do people say this to widows?

I've never heard it in reference to women whose husbands have died.

If this is true for men then it should be true for women, also. Do people say this in reference to single-fathers? Do people warn single fathers that their sons or daughters need a female role model to look up to? I've never heard it this way either.

I have several lesbian friends raising boys with their partners. Do I ever feel like their sons need a male role model? Nope. They all seem pretty happy.

I tried to think of exactly which personality traits came along with a Y-chromosome. Does one need a penis to be honorable? Trustworthy? Brave? Tender? Assertive?

Nope. I can't think of any personality traits that require a penis or male gender-identity.

What about statistics? Studies show that boys with no male role model grow up to be all kinds of horrible things.

But is it possible that the statistics are flawed? Let's just go on a mind-adventure, here. Is it *possible* that, under the stress of this ever-present idea that women can't teach boys how to be men, it is not the lack of penis or role-model that creates the problem but the lack of parenting confidence? It is a bit like going into a game with everyone telling you that you will fail and you will lose. That can shake your confidence, right? It might make you act in ways you normally wouldn't.

Maybe this is why some women are serial daters. Trying desperately to find that male role model because, you know, she's gonna ruin everything with her lack of penis and penis-appointed character traits, she introduces her kids to a host of less-than-suitable men. Perhaps if she felt like she was capable on her own, she wouldn't feel the *need* for the men in the first place, resulting in her creating high standards for herself and finding the *right* man only – not just *a* man.

I didn't feel the same panicked insecurity when it came to my girls. Wouldn't they need a male role model just as much?

I poked too many holes in this Truth. I didn't have anything to replace it, necessarily, but I certainly found enough wrong with it to set it aside and try to come up with a new, experimental Truth to replace it.

I thought about what traits it took to be a "good man."

Honors his word, follows through, protects those who can't protect themselves, speaks up when there is injustice or discrimination, takes care of his responsibilities, communicates his thoughts and feelings effectively, has healthy outlets for his stress, etc.

These are, really, just the traits it takes to be a good *human*. There is nothing about this list that reads *"penis necessary."*

And there were plenty of role models among our family and friends who embodied these traits.

By me repeatedly "making sure" Jack knew there was a male role model coming, not only was I assigning a gender to his activities (his two sisters were happy to build bows and arrows with him, why weren't they enough?) but I was also telling him he was different and things were going to be harder for just *him*...not the girls...just him.

I'm saying, "Since this will be harder for you, I'll bring in reinforcements."

That is unfair.

It is well-intended and it is subversively damaging.

I was *making* him needy and self-pitying. I was creating a need that may or may not have been there.

I decided, as an experiment, to back the hell off. And made sure I pointed out honorable traits in all of our friends and family, to him and his sisters, without attributing them to gender just to see what would happen.

And slowly but surely, he grew into his little Self. He started speaking up for himself more and apologizing less. He expresses himself clearly and openly. He stands up to the shit-head little neighborhood boys when he needs to and helps his little sister when she needs him. He doesn't do this because it's what "men" do. He does it because it's what people should do. Period.

I love parenting hacks, I tell ya.

And as an aside, this seems to work well with my girls, too. To quote Jaya, the oldest:

"I hate stupid tween memes with kids whining about their parents being divorced and having no male role model. I have tons! Nikola Tesla, Peeta, Stephen Hawking, The Doctor from Doctor Who, Sherlock, G-Dragon, Beast, Spiderman, Jack Skellington, Tony Stark, Michio Kaku, Neil deGrasse Tyson. Quit being victims, you bunch of punks. You embarrass me."

And speaking of kids...

My kids are really good at sensing when it's time to be a unit.

When I first first became a single mom, I explained to them that our little family was even more like a community.

They had jobs now and in order to afford the perks of our community, they had to contribute to make things go smoothly.

I am the Mayor. And the mayor doesn't pick up trash and heal sick people and work the cash register at the grocery store in her town. That's what the people in the community do. The mayor makes sure they have a good life for all that hard work and makes all the big hard decisions.

So anyway, the house is wrecked and I have a paper to write. I ran all over town today and I am tired. I took a short nap and just got up. I can hear all kinds of hustle-bustle in the living room. I thought they'd be asleep by now.

Instead all three kids are busying themselves with cleaning the house. They are just chatting away about whatever kids chat about, and unloading the dishwasher, and picking up the living room, and cleaning the bathroom.

They just *knew* the community wasn't going to function well without the house being clean so they just got to it. I didn't have to ask them. They didn't feel the need to inform me so they could get credit and praise. They just knew "okay, mom's occupied with important grownup stuff so let's do this so she has less to do."

I'm not the kind of humble person to say "I don't usually like to brag about my kids...." because I *do* like to brag about my kids. They've been through some upheavals, and instabilities, and been in some hostile environments, and less-than-functional environments, and they're really some relatively well-adjusted and cool little mofos.

And I don't have any tangible accomplishments except for them so I'm just gonna say it:

That's some damn fine parenting right there.

The Bridge – October 2013

I have spent the better part of the last year trying to build a community of single parents to act as a support group to each other. Initially, my heart and home was open to any and all.

If you were struggling, I'd find food and clothing and childcare and shelter and furniture for you. But I have since learned that nothing is that easy. I've had to turn my back and cover my ears a little.

If you need to join the tribe, you gotta cross the bridge.

I was high as hell on the movement I'd become a part of. Thanks to Facebook, single moms across the nation were connecting. Like *really* connecting and supporting each other. It had become my dream and life's mission to create a non-profit organization that connected single parents for co-housing, collection of goods, saving's circles, childcare share, and offer classes on car care, budgeting, parenting strategies.

I was going to make sure that single parents could parent alone with *dignity*, without help from the government and without the condescending pity or resentful vitriol that so many of us deal with. I've mentioned it before but we were really doing some shit. Like *big* shit. Moms were moving in together, shipping stuff across the country and even outside of the country. Some serious community magic was happening.

But...

That single mom I helped a few months ago?

I was friends with her on Facebook and, although she didn't go back to her ex, it was clear her priorities were skewed. It seemed she was more interested in having fun and reclaiming her lost youth than on getting her life together.

That was a little disappointing. I'm still glad we helped her, because she was on fire. But I'd be lying if I said I was satisfied with her progress.

That wasn't the only disappointment, either.

I also learned that it doesn't matter how idealistic or crunchy or well-intended a group of single parents are, people are still people.

I was a member of two online groups for single parent support. Both had aspirations of high connectedness. Both touted a spirit and environment of non-judgment. However, at the same time as if the drama gods were working overtime, both groups imploded and people revealed themselves. My local group was taken down by good intentions, hypersensitivity, and emotional anaphylaxis - initiated by two women who are not even single parents and both of them are my two closest friends.

The national group may still be operational but some drama unfolded over women judging each other for dating or screwing or something. I don't really know and didn't care. The group had ceased to serve me. I no longer felt like I could relate. My ex is not in my life causing courtroom drama. My children are far out of diapers.

Eventually a group of women, having confused me with another woman, created an offshoot group of which I became the topic of judgment and gossip. Bless their hearts.

All the glitter was gone. The truth revealed.

A crunchy group of women is still a group of women. And for some reason, no matter how connected to our higher selves we want to believe we are, we still revert to middle-school politics in groups.

No matter how flat you make your pancake, it's still got two sides. I think this is something Dr. Phil says but it's a good analogy and it applies.

I love all my friends deeply.

But when trading sob stories, it's best to keep in mind that there are stories not being told and stories not being heard. There are involved parties who are not present. No matter how much you think you know someone, you *don't* know them. You just don't. And that's when things get really hairy and really complicated. There is a shift in character and values when people are under extreme distress. And for some people, it feels like deception.

I don't think it's deception so much. I don't feel like anyone lied to me to get something out of me. I don't feel like anyone has purposely withheld information from me. But I do feel that people can't be expected to make rational decisions while the Universe is sticking needles under their fingernails.

When helping desperate people you accept a certain amount of risk. You accept that this person may turn on you - because they are desperate. Or they may use and use and use and never give back - because they are desperate. Or you may give and give and give and they will never help themselves - because they are desperate.

They are not conniving or shifty or sly. They are hurt people under stress and therefore cannot really be trusted to treat your love with the precious gentleness you think it deserves.

Also, eventually, everyone needs to cross the bridge.

I used to think my single moms and I were like survivors of a plane crash that landed in the ocean.

We hang desperately onto any piece of debris, with our babies clinging to our backs, gasping for air and watching out for sharks and praying someone comes to get us soon. But then, two of us decide to hang onto each other so we can take turns resting and neither sinks into the water. A third offers her makeshift bail bucket. A fourth joins and offers to paddle. And by pooling our resources and strengths we survive. But that's only half of it.

By working together we reach land. We walk together through the treacherous jungle evading wild animals and flesh eating bugs. We come to a deep canyon, a rickety bridge the only way across. On the other side of the gorge is a thriving village. They yell to us that there is plenty of food and plenty of shelter. If we make it across we will thrive. We just have to cross the bridge.

So some of us do.

We throw our kids on our back, adding weight and making the task even more dangerous. It's dangerous. It's unsteady. We tremble. We sweat. We cry. One wrong move and we fall to our death, taking our children with us. But we focus on the encouraging voices ahead and we will our limbs to move us despite our fear - leaving the untamed wild behind us. And having crossed we embrace each other and celebrate. We take our places at the fire. We warm ourselves and our children. We fill our bellies.

And sitting by the fire, we notice that our numbers are smaller. Not everyone made it across. We have left some behind.

They are at the gorge, paralyzed with fear.

They pray that Tarzan will vine-swing in to rescue them.
Or
They are angry that we left them behind, and shout curses at us.
Or
They scream for help and want us to come back over and aid them across.

But we can't. And it's not because we don't want to. But we've already done it and we can't risk our lives for them. They *have* to do this alone.

We're on the safe side with open arms and a hut and some coconut water and a seat by the fire waiting patiently, hollering encouragement, or angrily barking instructions on how to safely cross.

And sometimes we have to watch as the tigers consume them before they get the courage to move, or we watch them succumb to famine, or we watch them hesitate a little too long causing the bridge to give, allowing them and their children to tumble and perish.

And we feel helpless but there is nothing we can do.

Some days I wish I could grow wings and grab all these women and carry them to safety.

But I don't have wings and I've already dragged them panicked and gasping from the water to the shore.

And now it's time for my children and me to learn how to forage and build fires and huts and fish and hunt so we can pull our own weight in the new village.

And we try our best to be grateful for our survival and push down the nightmares of those we lost on the bridge.

Fuck Up

I fucked up.

I went back to college at the top of Fall.

I did very, very poorly in college the first time around, not because the work was difficult, but because I had way too much freedom. I didn't go to class ever, and I didn't withdraw either, so my GPA is the absolute worst.

Thankfully, I got accepted to a local community college. I'd heard it was a terrible school but I didn't really care. I just need some credentials. I know I'm smart. I know I work hard. But no employer really has any reason to believe that if I don't have some kind of paper to back it up.

I realized sometime this summer, quite suddenly, that I didn't want to live in Mobile forever.

I don't want to live in America forever, actually.

I always wanted to travel; so I decided I needed to find a way to get a degree, and then I'd have a better chance of landing a job abroad. I know I have a long way to go with my terrible GPA but slow progress is still progress.

Well...

When I went to register I found that a schedule had already been produced for me. The class times were terrible, but my grandmother offered to watch the kids so it was okay. As long as I was in.

My first class was at 8 am and on the first day the professor didn't show up until 9:30.

See, I'm under the impression that if I'm paying for something then I'm getting something in return. I don't appreciate paying someone to teach me and driving across town for some idiot to la-dee-da into class an hour and a half late.

So...

I told him as much.

I'm not a child. I'm not a 15-year-old; this is not high school.

This is college. I'm paying out-of-pocket because I don't quality for any financial aid. I am paying the school for him to *teach me*. That is his *job*.

Well, we eventually worked through that together, and I did well in his class. However, the kids were miserable at my grandma's house.

I told them to suck it up. Means to an end and all that...

My other class was a drafting class with a super mellow teacher. He was very nice but unfortunately the school hadn't ordered the proper textbooks. Because of the updates in the software we were supposed to learn, the updated textbooks were absolutely essential. Because of a miscommunication between the staff and the school, there were no old textbooks available for us to use. So he did his best teaching us, on a whiteboard, how to use a computer drafting program.

Most days, defeated, he sent us home early.

While he was lovely, as a person and as a teacher, I was constantly aware of the time and gas wasted driving across town only to discover, day after day, that I wasn't going to learn anything.

My third class....

That one was in the evening and I paid CBL's oldest to come watch the kids. So if I'm paying for a sitter *and* gas and for the class itself the *last* thing I want to hear on the first day is:

"Okay y'all, listen up. I don' wanna be here an' I know y'all don' neither. E'rybody gon' git an A up in dis class because I hate gradin' papers. All the tes' gon' be open book. Okay? Good."

Everyone else nodded with excitement that they got a "good" teacher because apparently "good" means lazy as fuck and insulting to my time.

Suck it up, Jess. Means to an end.

So the first day started with her reading straight from the text. Typical classroom stuff. Then, for some reason, she got on the subject of chromosomes and she said – for real – that if someone has a Y- chromosome they are a man, and if a woman has two Y chromosomes then she is a lesbian. If a man has three X chromosomes then he is gay.

She said this.

Honestly.

Like, she wasn't being funny or ironic.

And all these twits in class start laughing.

Then she tells a story about her "gay ackin'" nephew and how her sister hugs him too much and it's making him a sissy.

It's as this point that I realize this school lives down to its reputation.

Then she makes us watch this psychotic video of this ex-football player turned preacher barking aggressively about how Beyoncé is famous because she doesn't eat or sleep. She works hard toward her goals and that people are too lazy.

We were asked to give our opinion on what the preacher said. I said that while I understand that he is trying to motivate people, it's unhealthy to encourage Americans to ignore their health and well-being. Additionally, success does not look the same to everyone. My version of success is not necessarily monetary and it's a good thing everyone is different.

She told me I missed the point.

Maybe so.

I sent her an email directly that evening telling her that I was very uncomfortable with her discussion about her nephew, and her many references to government checks and food stamps as I was unsure what they had to do with psychology.

She apologized for my being offended and said she was just trying to lighten the mood.

I said okay.

After that day, however, everyone got the notes she'd emailed the night before, but me.

I was starting to think I'd made a huge mistake.

I called the Counselor to see if I could change majors and, by extension, all my classes. She said it was too late but after talking to me on the phone decided I was worth some extra effort and string-pulling. It was, apparently, merely hours from the end of the last day to withdraw and get your money back. She called this and that office, touted my AP English and ACT score. She was shocked at how things had gone so far and "didn't wanna lose this one." But alas, her efforts were to no avail.

I could continue to pay for gas and not learn anything. Even if I changed majors, two of the three classes would not apply. Or I could withdraw and at least get my time back.

I went to the office and withdrew. I did not get my money back. I just fucked it all up. Just fucked over here and fucked over there.

Maybe I should have stayed? I don't know.

I'm applying to different schools now and I'll try again for next semester however this time I think I'll do online classes only. I don't do well in a classroom environment...obviously.

Reboot.
Again.

Amnesia

Even now, several years beyond my divorce, I get hints from people I love about who I was before all of it happened. Recovering from a dysfunctional relationship is like recovering from amnesia.

Typically, while digging out of the bad marriage mud pit, I wasn't particularly concerned with remembering who I am.

I was focused on creating who I *want* to be.

But while visiting with Jenn and discussing how I decide what to make for dinner she noted my enthusiasm:

"THAT'S what you should write. You should write a *cookbook.* Food seems to be such a part of your story. You told me how you learned to cook from being a latch-key kid. Then you could afford the good stuff and you ate well. Then you were broke and had to figure out how to satisfy that desire for artful food on a single-mom budget. I never realized it until now!"

Yeah.

Food *was* a big part of my "story." Food was my *thing* for a long, long time. The sensation was so strange. It was like someone telling me who I was "before the accident."

I feel so removed from myself sometimes. So much of me got lost in the fire.

But instead of rummaging through the burning ashes of what was a beautiful house and finding a photo album or a treasured stuffed animal, I find personality traits and hobbies that I used to possess but forgot to grab when I ran from the flames.

I used to love to cook. I really, really loved to cook. I used to own ramekins and I used them regularly. I used them to make coconut caramel crème brûlée until the blowtorch I used to caramelize the sugar was used as a lighter for lighting cigarettes and was left outside in the rain.

Then I couldn't make the things I wanted to make anymore.

I had a cupcake business before cupcakes became ubiquitous and trendy. But I had to stop the business because my ex wanted to change careers and someone had to go get a "real job."

It's so distant.

The real tragedy of this sort of amnesia is that I remember that cooking is something I used to enjoy. I remember cooing at the Williams-Sonoma store window. I remember crying when I unwrapped the immersion blender my sister bought me for Christmas. I remember the sublime ecstasy I experienced when I ate my first Vosges candy bar.

But, like any good amnesic soap opera saga, none of that is part of who I am now. I don't love to cook anymore. It's actually a chore. I do it because I want to feed my kids well and develop their palates, but I'd always prefer *not* to. And it hurts and confuses me a little. I don't know how something that used to be such a huge part of my identity could turn to ash so quickly.

And people who knew me before talk to me as if perfecting an authentic mole sauce is still something I am interested in doing.

And it's just gone.

Delivery

You wanna know why I haven't dated much since I got divorced?

Because I am receiving so much love, all the time, from my friends and family that I just don't need to.

I've been feeling pissy today with all the college crap and I have two-thirds of a bottle of wine in my belly, but just now the doorbell rang.

I opened it and there was a bag of clothes and a note that said

"Jessica, you look cold. Quick put this on!"

From Anonymous.

Inside the bag were some cute tops and sweaters!

Shopping for myself is at the bottom of my priority list so it's sort of always something I need. I *always* need clothes.

And one of my lovely lady friends just blessed me with some stuff and it is literally impossible for me to feel bad.

Man oh man, I've gathered some good ones over the years.

Mask

"Turtle frown" and "super pout" and "stank face"...

Even though I felt like I'd taken great strides in finally allowing myself to be photographed, it was a blog reader who pointed out that I'm still in hiding.

And so begins the next big dig...

I was at one of many random weekly social home school engagements when I introduced myself to a woman who'd already recognized me from my blog.

She and I and a few other moms chatted for about a half an hour before the one who recognized me interrupted me:

"I hope you don't mind me saying this, but you are really pretty."

I felt extremely flattered because just that morning I had a mirror war in which I chastised myself for getting so fat and for my favorite jeans not fitting and for my hair looking a mess. I'd literally contemplated shaving it off that morning. For real. She continued:

"But, I gotta be honest. I hardly recognized you because you're always making faces in your pictures. Like frowning and stuff. It really doesn't do you justice."

She's right. I always make some stank face in my pictures. "Stank face" is my "duck face" as it were.

"Yeah," I answered, "but that's just me being silly."

"Hmm," she peered at me, "I think it's you hiding."

WHO ARE YOU, WIZARD!?! STOP LOOKING INTO MY SOUL!!!

It stung a bit but usually when something stings it's because there is a little barb of truth.

What started as a compliment was now suddenly making me really uncomfortable. Not because she was prying or that small talk had suddenly turned into therapy. More because she was right and it's one of those dinosaurs I wasn't ready to excavate yet.

I do have a bunch of issues with being perceived as "pretty." I used to be concerned with and occupied with being the most attractive girl and, really, it got me into a lot of trouble. That was when I was young and dumb. I didn't primp, per se, but I definitely wanted to be looked at.

Now I don't like to be looked at. I like to be *heard*.

When I was a pretty girl I was leered at and preyed upon. I got attention from cute boys but when I think about the creepy stares and lip smacks and cat calls from greasy old men, starting as early as eleven and twelve years old, my blood boils.

Now I'm a loud girl and people listen to me. People don't say "Jessica's so hot" anymore. People say "Jessica's smart/funny/wise/childish/ridiculous/got some issues/is abrasive." I like all of those over "pretty" or "hot." "Pretty" and "hot" are not character traits. They are symmetry and balance resulting from a favorable round of genetic roulette. They really have nothing to do with *me. Inside.*

When I was a pretty girl I thought I liked being a pretty girl. Really, I'd just become a sexual object and just sort of went with it. Attention was attention.

Then I got plump and people started listening to me and noticing *me* and I realize I greatly prefer it. But now I don't know how to be visible without feeling unsafe.

I just got punched in the face by my next big Issue. I am *terrified* of being considered pretty because it reminds me of being young and being taken advantage of and I don't want to give anyone an excuse not to listen to me ever again.

There was an episode of Doctor Who where there was a hotel and in each room was the occupants' biggest fear. Given the stomach knots, heart palpitations and juicy eyeballs I'm experiencing while trying to write this, I'd be willing to bet that inside my room would be me at 130 pounds wearing a cute outfit and with my hair done.

I know, intellectually, that as a full-grown adult with boundaries and well-honed social skills I could keep myself physically and emotionally safe. But being attractive is so deeply hardwired to be associated with "danger" "trouble" and "not being taken seriously" that I have a hard time feeling favorably toward the possibility. Additionally, it *feels* like there is an either/or choice.

I know it isn't true. But among ladies it *feels* like you can't be pretty *and* smart *and* approachable. It feels like you always have to choose two. You can be pretty and smart, but you'll be intimidating and alienate people. You can be smart and approachable, but probably because you're not *too* pretty. Or you can be pretty and approachable because other people think they're smarter than you.

I know, intellectually, this isn't true. I can name lots of women who are smart, pretty and approachable. But something deep in me sort of thinks that won't apply to me.

I feel like I've been performing. I've been zany and goofy and a loose cannon and brash and tell-it-like-it-is as a technique for disarming people. All of that *is* a part of me but I feel like I crank it up when I meet new people so they *know* I'm down-to-Earth right away.

I hide behind this blog because I can just say what I want to say and say what's real and true without having to make you comfortable first. I live online to reveal the real me with all the thoughts and feelings and flaws and grump. I can't count how many female friends said to me, back in the pretty days, "You know, when I first met you I thought you'd be stuck up because you're pretty but you're actually really cool."

Uh....

Well, shit.

So I act like a bumbling fart of a person to just get the disarming part over and done with so we can get to being friends. I exaggerate my ogre-ness in order to cut straight to getting real. How's that for backwards?

But back then, when I *was* "pretty" I did it by being vulgar and brash. Now I do it by being chubby and having Beetlejuice hair. I keep weight on because chubby black women are associated with warmth and wisdom. I keep it on because it keeps men away. I keep it on because it helps me avoid thinking about all of *this*.

It's baffling, when I step outside myself, how something so innocuous and out of my control creates so much shame and guilt and fear.

I feel shame because I feel like attention for being pretty is attention I don't deserve. I didn't *do* anything. It's not an accomplishment.

I feel guilt because I feel like I should embrace and enjoy it and make the most of it. Like I won't be 31 forever and I'm a young looking 31. I should probably appreciate it more.

I feel fear most of all, though. Attention from men straight up paralyzes me. I am afraid of men. Genuinely. And as long as I am fat and nappy-haired they pretty much leave me alone and I don't have to deal with them.

Some of the most painful things I've experienced have been a direct result of my being attractive and appealing, and not having the words or framework to create a clear boundary. Almost all the painful things, actually.

I'm fighting a hard-wired, visceral, PTSD-like fear. And it's real. I feel it in my body. My throat closes and my chest feels tight. It's not some random tape I've just gotten used to believing. It's a real, live demon. My means of defense - aside from being fat and fuzzy - has been kind of acting like a "bro" when I meet guys.

Typically, they only see that side of me. The bawdy nerd in shlumpy baggy clothes. I *am* a bawdy nerd. But I'm *also* a total softie romantic and really malleable and snuggly and sweet and bubbly.

I wouldn't dare let any of *them* know that. I'm way too scared and, based on results, I have no reason *not* to be.

I know that at some point my desire to feel love will have to overcome my fear, and I hate that dealing with this shit is probably the first step to getting there.

Ugh...

I was high on dealing with my issues for a while and took a big break and felt like "Welp I'm all done making myself a better person" and meanwhile My Personal Vulnerability Issues were tapping me on the shoulder and saying *ahem* "I'll just be sitting over here when you're ready."

Well, I'm not ready, but I think the random woman I met is serving as a catalyst from the Universe. So here *this* shit goes.

Selfies

I've been taking a lot of selfies lately to get myself used to my face and to see what my face does when I'm not distorting it.

It's like exposure therapy.

I know it's commonly perceived as being egotistical, but I kind of need it right now so I can just get comfortable with how I look.

I'm not thin anymore. I look the way I look. And it's okay.

Santa – December 2013

These struggles and my writing have connected me with brilliant bold women across the country. And right now, just for shiggles, we are all playing Santa.

This isn't a soul-opening piece. This is just about friendship and commonality and community.

I've been friends, both virtual and in-person, with a group of women from around the world. Some are married, some are single, some are single moms. But all are giving, open-minded, honest, respectful and emotionally mature and willing to grow. They have become one of the only soft places I have to land.

Usually we just gather online to vent about ex-husbands, children, boyfriends or talk movies or feminism or share pics of hot men. But we decided to do something amazing. We are playing Secret Santa.

So this year while some of us are painting on smiles for our children, or some of us are bullied by in-laws, or some of us are painfully single we have something to look forward to - some small connective love token from a soul sister miles away.

Some of us have never even met but we are sending boxes of love across hundreds or thousands of miles for each other.

I got my secret Santa assignment and can't wait to find or make a special gift for her.

This weekend was particularly rough mentally for me so to have solace in a group of women who aren't using me as their token wise black woman, who challenge me and help me grow means more than the world to me.

I spent the morning having stress-related chest pains and, with my Santa assignment, get to end my day with a smiling heart.

Candyman

You came by and I made you something sweet. That does not mean I'm a candyman.
Something strange happened recently as a result of my blog and I'm going to try my best to express how it makes me feel.

So in recent weeks a lot lot LOT of people have called me for advice or support. Most of these people only know me through virtual means through the blog or through Facebook. One woman in particular came to me for some advice about her life and I gave it to her. She didn't like it and proceeded to call me a fraud for my "love and light" image that she felt was apparently false.

Mmmk, let's just get something straight while we're all here.

I have always written for *me*. My marriage, my divorce, my kids and I were on fire. I had nowhere to put my feelings so I started a blog and put my them into the ether so that they were out of my body. I chose a public forum because a friend of mine had a blog after her divorce and reading about *her* experiences made me feel less alone. That is the most I hoped for my blog.

What I did *not* intend was to become is a life coach.

I feel like some people find some blog posts particularly wise and then they say "oh wow, Jessica Vivian is a wise woman and she's brown and that feels like a hug. I will seek her out any time I need strength and comfort"

But I'm just a person with my own wagon of nonsense to pull. Jenn helped me work it out in metaphor and because I love metaphors I'll share it now:

So let's say I'm just a little chef in a meat pie shop making delicious meat pies every day. Then one day a customer comes in while I just *happen* to be making myself some candy because I've had a crap day and I need some.

I decide to share some of the candy with the customer and the customer leaves and, despite having walked into a *meat pie* shop, assumes I'm a candyman.

This person goes and tells all her friends how great the candy shop is and just dreams about how great the candy is. As far as the customer is concerned I am Willy fucking Wonka.

So the customer comes back with money in hand to buy some candy.

But I don't have any because I'm a chef who makes meat pies. The meat pies are great. But the customer is *angry* at me for not selling her some candy.

That is what I've been dealing with. People who choose to elevate me to Sensei levels who are *angry* with me when I'm not the ever-available "Mother Earth of Wisdom" that they needed. Or I'm too contradictory and it annoys them. A sad side product of being open-minded enough to be willing to change your opinion when new evidence presents itself is that you always look wishy-washy. My words are scanned and I am appointed to positions and put into boxes without my consent by people I do not know.

On *their* end, through reading all my thoughts, they feel a closeness that I don't get to feel on my end. But they forget that.

So some near-*stranger* will want me, their personal Jiminy Cricket, to coach them through their relationship problems and when I am not as funny or warm or maternal or wise or as they expected they get angry.

Angry.
And go rant on their Facebook statuses about how mean I am.

Je ne comprends pas.

But there is a lot about humans I "ne comprends pas" so I'll just keep making my meat pies because they are savory and delicious and fulfilling to *me* and I'll even keep sharing my candy. And the next time some angry woman gets my job confused I will shove a meat pie into her entitled face.

The Groom

This is a cautionary tale about a predator, but not the kind of predator you think.

As a single mom, I am well-versed in the methodology of sexual predators. I am hyper-aware of the act of grooming.

For those who don't have children, grooming is the act of taking specific action to establish closeness, trust and emotional connection with someone to make it easier to abuse that person. But I generally thought, as I think many women do, that grooming was an act that was reserved for sexual predators only.

I never, ever believed or was trained to believe that it was possible to be groomed by a friend and yet, that is exactly what me and about forty other women recently experienced.

I have written before about my Facebook group.

Originally, I was in a Facebook group for single parents.
We lamented our single-ness but, more importantly, we saved each other's asses.

There was one member, however, who caused the hairs on everyone's neck to stand up and whose histrionic episodes caused the group to implode.
I refused to let that stop me from giving love.

After struggling so much in the beginning of my single parent journey I vowed to myself that NO woman or man connected to me, who is a single parent, would struggle so needlessly. I would find a way to soften the blow.

So I started *another* group on Facebook and the love and goodwill started anew.

There was one member in particular, however, who raised the hairs on the back of my neck the same way the other woman (who I'd recently friend-divorced) did.

She was so sweet and seemed so fragile. I'd never met her, in real life, but she seemed to really see something in me that she needed. She called me her "machete mama," a reference to when I wrote about how single parents are like castaways on a deserted island hacking their way through the jungle. Someone's up front, with a machete, cutting down brush and clearing a path. I guess, in her mind, that was me. And while that title felt burdensome, I didn't mind being someone's champion.

I never mind.

Which makes me the perfect magnet for personality disorders.

But despite this sweet, idyllic long-distance friendship there *were* things that, for lack of a better term, skeeved me out.

She told me she loved me often, which was creepy. Despite having the group to share in, she would always text me directly with her problems, which felt like an invasion into my life and space. She planned a trip to stay at my home despite us having never met. We did video chat once, which was nice, but she was oddly familiar with me during our chat. At one point she panned the computer and was not wearing pants. She responded with a casual "whoops."

She wanted to video chat because she needed advice on whether or not to involve herself in the criminal prosecution of her former rapist. She also shared with me the details of said rape, which was possibly the second most horrifying rape story I've ever heard, with a kind of detached casualness that I found odd.

But, I've never been raped so I thought maybe it was some sort of normal dissociation that happened with rape victims.

Anyway, a few days before Christmas I received a text that she'd been raped again by the same guy. Her story was that he'd found out she'd been involved in this whole legal rape case and singled her out and punished her by raping her again. She sent me a picture of the choke marks and bruises around her neck.

Naturally, I was in a panic.

But I was very confused as to why she *just* told me.

I thought, if she is in real pain or danger why wouldn't she call on the emotional support of the *entire* fifty-woman group?

But, because of the severity of the situation and the picture of the bruises any small, itchy doubts were quickly pushed aside.

One of my friends was hurting. One of my friends was in danger. One of my friends was in a hospital – alone.

All I could think was "How can I make it better?"

I urged her to share with the group. She did, even posting the picture of her bruises with the headline "Trigger Warning". And the group, as I expected, showered her with emotional support immediately.

> *How could this happen?*
> *Where are the police?*
> *Why is it taking so long to get a rape kit done?*
> *Where is your family?*

We were all consumed.

Completely *consumed* with this woman, her rape and her pain.

However, the next day I received a shocking email from one of the ladies in my group. She was trying to find a way to send money and this woman was not answering any texts or phone calls. She decided to look the woman up online to see if she could find any leads that would help her contact her.

And that's when all hell broke loose.

This woman, as it turned out, was a *world-renowned* internet hoax artist.

Just typing her name in a search engine led to about a dozen websites dedicated to warning people and exposing her lies.

This woman faked a rape, faked HIV, faked cancer.

She went so far as to *shave her head* and *order hospital gowns* to solidify her story.

She accepted *thousands* of dollars from people concerned with this young woman and her harrowing story of survival. And she was about to do it again.

It wasn't just my group, but there was another group – centered mostly on Attachment Parenting single moms – that was also in the process of setting up a foundation or donation site for her.

Confusion. Hurt. Rage.

All of these things invaded the minds and hearts of the women in my group.

I was mostly wildly shocked and entertained.

The whole hullabaloo was like a reality-show train wreck.

I asked the group how the situation should be handled and the general consensus was that, whether the current rape was real or not, the group no longer felt like a safe space and she should leave.

I eliminated her from the group. When she confronted me I told her exactly why.

"Someone in the group Googled you so we could find a way to contact you and we found all your hoax stuff. The trust is broken. I wish you well but you have to go."

The source of the drama was gone. I dusted my virtual hands and believed we were done with it. But we weren't even close to done with it.

The *source* of the pain was gone but something insidious took root.

The infiltration and antics of the notorious lying woman caught everyone off guard.

Once I removed her from the group, I assumed it was back to business as usual.

I assumed wrong.

That same day I got three messages from women in the group:

"_____ *raises my red flags.*"

"How well do you know _____?"

"I think you should get rid of everyone you don't know personally."

"Maybe we should run everyone through Google, just to be safe."

And just like that, where one seat sat empty Suspicion was more than happy to settle in and get comfortable.

Literally *weeks* after we were all high on camaraderie, sending each other Christmas gifts on what is usually the most sickeningly lonely time of the year for single moms, we'd grown cynical and mistrustful.

My sole opportunity for social interaction was crumbling before my eyes, dying of infection.

But when I stepped outside myself to find out *why* this was happening, the gravity and the cruelty of what this woman does became clear.

Again, aside from the occasional unwanted grope from my nightclubbing days I have never been sexually assaulted. But many, many women in my group have.

And if you are a single mother, mentally ill or not, who thrives on stealing money and attention from large groups of people, what better target than a group of single mothers, a third of whom have been victims of sexual abuse?

This woman sat among us long enough for us to get comfortable enough to share our experiences and our truths and she used them against us. As one of my friends stated, "We had a safe place, we had trust, and she violated that trust and essentially built a stage on our *backs* so she could act out her shit."

A Predator.

In the days that followed the ousting, while still fielding emails about who is real and who is fake and who is suspicious, slowly women began to share their feelings on what had happened.

This liar made one critical mistake in her almost flawless performance.

After posting pictures of her "bruises" from the hospital, she sent a second picture of herself "feeling better" with this bizarre watered-down smile on her face. I had no compass as to whether or not this was normal behavior but for all the women in the group who *had* been raped or sexually assaulted, this was the blaring alarm.

But we didn't question her in that moment because no one wants to be the person to question the validity of the traumatic event – a traumatic event that was still so real and so raw for so many.

24 hours worth of this woman's drama undid years and years of emotional safety for my friends. This incident opened wounds, reignited nightmares, revived anxiety and paranoia. It was PTSD for them.

Getting rid of the problem didn't end the problem at all. What this woman did is more vile and more insidious than I could have imagined.

I believed, like so many people do, that the anonymity of the internet provided some sort of buffer to real-life emotional damage and the kids who got caught up in some silly Catfish drama were exactly that – naive kids. She is in her early 20s so, to me, she's a "naive kid."

But she was a naive kid who had the power to unsettle the lives and hearts of who knows how many across the country over her years and years as a con artist. And she impacts not just the women she touches directly, but victims of sexual abuse – period.

Women like her only further perpetuate the slut-shaming and victim blaming that keeps 97% of all rapists OUT of JAIL.

The seeds of mistrust and doubt have been planted.

I hurt so deeply for my friends.

I always have words, but for the way I feel about what this snake has done to my friends' hearts I have none.

I have none.

On how everyone will cope with the frothing of painful memories, the digging up of buried hurt, I can only hope for swift and effective emotional growth and peace. I felt for a while, since the group was *mine*, that somehow this was *my* fault. Maybe I didn't vet people well enough. And this is the second person with a personality disorder that has slithered their way into my inner circle. What's wrong with *me* that this keeps happening?

A friend answered that question well:

"You don't attract crazies. You attract **people**. **People** want to be around you and statistically, some of those people are going to be crazy."

So here's my ultimate takeaway from all this madness:

Firstly, drawing emotionally vampiric personality disorder people is not an indication that something is *wrong* with me – or you – or any of us who has dealt with one of a handful of these types. If anything, it's an indication that there are some things about you that are really, really *right*.

It means you are empathetic, helpful, big-hearted and strong. You fight aggressively, teeth bared, for those who are hurting and need a champion. That is not something to be ashamed of and it's not something to allow a few assholes to take away from you.

Secondly, there *is* no completely safe place because *humans– no forum, no Facebook group, no self-help club – any and all bonding and sharing is at the risk of being hurt. All human closeness involves an element of emotional danger. But that's the risk we take.*

I can hear some of my happily-marrieds disagreeing with me but I also know many, many happily-marrieds who learned the hard and painful way that sometimes even your "safe place" is contaminated without your knowing.

I've gotten more *good* back from my investments in humans than bad. I'm not afraid of a little risk. A couple bad returns aren't slowing me down.

The best I can do is continue to draw my boundaries with a permanent marker. I used to be terrible at this. I had *no* boundaries. I used to pride myself on "having never thrown anyone away." Now, honestly, I am most impressed with my ability to say "no" without feeling the need to explain myself.

Despite all the hurt everyone is coping with, ultimately I am *proud* of us, some of us having narrowly escaped marriages to poisonous, vampire people for trusting our Spidey senses and being swift and decisive.

Jessica a year ago would have wanted to hear her side and work it out and try to play devil's advocate. I still have no way of knowing if *this* rape was a real or fake one.

Jessica *now* trusts her gut, takes action and lets it go. It doesn't matter if it is real or fake. There are plenty of resources available for her. She has a family. *I* don't have to be the human band-aid.

The group is still fractured now. People still feel unsafe and there's nothing I can do to change or alleviate that and it's not my responsibility to. But like all wounds, hopefully, this one will heal and we will all be stronger and smarter from it.

Brick Wall

This is a the writing of a mad black woman.
So, let me start with the bad news.

I was rejected today from a college I applied to.
Now let me explain why this news is pretty close to making me pull a crazy right now.
This decision not to accept me is based on my transcripts from the last time I was in college which was over thirteen years ago. Thirteen years ago, I didn't want to be in college so I screwed around and flunked a lot. I faked wanting to go back a couple of times only to withdraw. Then I met my ex and had a bunch of kids and a crappy marriage.

Now, I'm a grown ass woman. I've got three kids and no education. Now I know *exactly* what I want to do. I want to teach abroad. I want to travel and, most of all, I want to show my kids that I can do this.

Nothing, on Earth, is more important to me than my kids seeing me, as an individual. achieve at least *one fucking goal*.

My oldest daughter is almost eleven. I am past the halfway mark. I *need* to be in and out of school ASAP because I *NEED* to feel like I contributed to her financial security at some point before she leaves my house.

The whole time I was married we bounced from home to home, following the lead of "the man of the house" who barely managed to keep a roof over us but always managed to have cigarettes or alcohol at his disposal.

So I left.

And despite being intellectually impressive and effervescent, I worked mid-range hospitality or office jobs with hourly pay. I never made enough to cover after school care or a baby sitter so that I could work full time or get health insurance and somehow, even with an ex-husband with *no* schedule in the *same city*, I didn't have his support to watch *his own* children so I could work.

So I ran away home and things have been better. We have food and shelter. And that's great. But, my mom and sister are doing the bulk of the financial supporting. My ex does none. My contribution to our well-being, as agreed upon by my mom and I, was going to college and getting my degree so that I can get out of this tar pit and stay out.

I don't want to be on welfare. I don't want to rely on family.

I need to move forward.

I just recently identified that my complete apathy and disconnection from myself was depression.

I'm a little depressed. I've gone numb. This *waiting* period was killing me. But what kept me from letting it consume me was the *hope* that I was going back to school, again, in the Spring. I knew that the interim was temporary, so I could trudge forward.

I had a *plan*.

I just had to wait for my "yes."

And today, completely by surprise, in the mail with Christmas cards and my water bill was a big, fat No.

No.

It doesn't matter how hungry, how competent, how focused, how determined you are.

You are just the academic footprint you made when you were eighteen and stupid and directionless.

Rejection.

And I cried today...

Which would be the first time since May when my ex-husband failed to call his child on her birthday.

I felt like I'd been shot. Or hit by a train. The carrot was yanked away. I sobbed in the bathroom. Then my best friend called and I sobbed again. Then I read an encouraging text from another friend and sobbed some more.

I'm crestfallen.

There is no other word.

So now the money I was going to spend on Christmas presents is just going to college applications and transcripts.

The kids' gifts are covered by my family and they already knew mommy couldn't get them anything and assumed Daddy wouldn't.

The reason I'd only applied to one school was because I could only *afford* to apply to one. When you have no income, no alimony and no child support - $50 is a lot of money.

I have an ice pick in my chest - the stress has a distinct feeling.

I am in a panic.

I just really don't have the *time* to wait another semester to start school.

Like I said, I'm already more than halfway done with the child raising.

So I finally get my shit together when she's an adult? What good is that?

I need this piece of paper *YESTERDAY*.

I know I screwed up.

I should never have moved to Tampa. I sure as shit should have never spoken to him. I picked a terrible husband. I shoulda just stayed in school. I know I know I know...

But I *didn't*.

And I feel like I'm cleaning up my act.

I have completely devoted myself to my children. I'm not one of those moms still chasin' fairies in the field.

Party time is over... has *been* over...

I dove right in to parenthood and never looked back.

When I got divorced I didn't wipe my tears with someone's penis.

My one and *only* goal is being a contributing member of society for my children.

Dating and sex really don't factor in to that plan and, therefore, are a waste of my time.

I cannot *possibly* be more focused on bettering myself.

SO...

WHAT IS THIS SHIT, UNIVERSE!?!?!??!

Do NOT do this to me right now.

Do. Fucking. NOT.

Universe, if you were a person I would grab you by your throat and snarl right in your face and tell you straight up:

"I am NOT the one to mess with right now. You get back in line and you do what I need you to do. Period."

But the Universe is not a person so the rage coursing through my veins has nothing to do but make my chest hurt and make my throat close and give me a headache.

I have two kids to look after tonight so I can't go on a bender. I don't do drugs. I am sick to death of eating my feelings. So I just have to sit here and BE angry and heartbroken.

I find this to be an inconvenience.

I know I'll get through this because, let me tell you, I am fueled by pure rage now.

RAGE.

How DARE the Universe slow me down? I don't know who the Universe thinks he is.

I need a bat.

I need a bat and a room full of fine china.

I want to TEAR something APART right now.

And I want to rage cry.

Actually, I know exactly what I want to do. I want to take a bat to my CAR which is leaking transmission fluid all over Mobile, Alabama every time I leave my house...

So I don't leave my house...

So add a little cabin fever to that rage and you got me right now, nostrils flared, eyes wild and hungry for blood.

You hear that, Universe? You messed with the wrong one, today. I know I messed up and you proved your point. But "Jessica Vivian" is NOT going down as a cautionary tale, you hear me?

That was the married Jessica with no spine. Jessica *Vivian* is back....

I don't think you understand.

Jessica Vivian has giant, stainless steel balls. And Jessica Vivian don't take no shit. And Jessica

Vivian is big-hearted and patient but nooooo one wants to get on Jessica Vivian's bad side.

And now, Universe, you just made yourself an enemy. You think you can slow me down with this college rejection trick?

You. Fucking. Watch. Me.

"Jessica Vivian" is the machete mama.
I'm trying to show all the single mamas that it doesn't matter how long it's been, how many babies they got, how beat down they were – *no one* and *nothing* can take their dreams away without their permission.

My dreams ain't budging so you get on board, Universe, or we are gonna have some serious problems.

I'm gonna sell all this crap I got lying around and I'm gonna CLEP outta some classes because I'm fucking brilliant, maybe you forgot. I'm gonna be in class by midterm this Spring. I'm *going* to get my education and I am *going* abroad. Deal. With. That.

J. Viv, out.

mic drop

Christmas Doctor Who Seafood

Christmas was good. We had a bunch of seafood because something about Jesus...
I don't remember what the tie-in was. I just planted myself in front of the snow crab legs and ate my pain.
We had a Doctor Who themed Christmas tree with a weeping angel tree-topper. For those who do not speak Whovian, it's a statue of an angel that moves when you blink or look away. If it catches up to you it could kill you or zap you back in time and steal your energy or something like that.
Y'know, spirit of Christmas.

Sword

The post where I get New Age on you but trust me, it's worth it.

So, as you know I experienced a pretty weighty setback recently.

Being denied to this school was aggressively painful because, as I said in the post, to get tripped up at the beginning of the race just seriously stung. I could taste the mud.

And someone once told me that anger is pain turned inside out.

And I was angry.

I was trembling angry and all I could think about was getting a bat and smashing everything. And swearing loudly

Every time I closed my eyes I saw hot, burning anger and me – engulfed in flames – eyes wild and holding a bat looking frantically for something to hit.

It was fuel.

I could feel myself becoming addicted to it.

The anger, I felt, was what was going to help me move forward.

But I knew that throwing my anger at the Universe would eventually catch the eye of my step-mom and "spirit guide" and sure enough, bright and early this morning, I got a phone call.

I almost didn't answer because I knew what was coming and frankly, I didn't want to go there.

I wanted to hold on to the rage fire. It was the only fuel available and I feared that if I wasn't angry, I wouldn't be productive.

But I picked up the phone.

Allow me to detour for a moment because I want to talk about what *I* think a consciousness shift is.

I think people only hold on to thoughts and habits that work for them – even destructive, harmful thoughts and habits. It depends on your "agenda."

If your "agenda" is to avoid emotional pain then you may self-harm in physical ways that help detour that pent up energy but also distract you from feeling your feelings. Because the worst thing you can imagine experiencing is your feelings.

You get it?

For example, someone who smokes knows the data. They know it's bad for them. They may even want to quit. But if, in the moment, their stress level goes beyond their coping strategy the only agenda is "relieve stress" and all that knowledge doesn't matter. It's time for a smoke.

A shift in consciousness happens when your agenda dies and "the tape" stops playing.

It's that one day the smoker says "the stress won't kill me, I can manage it." And they do, and they can.

Those harmful habits and coping methods are kinda like walking around in full rain gear just in case it rains. But it's sunny out.

What happens if you peek out from under your umbrella and notice the sun? Suddenly, that snow gear feels silly and useless and burdensome.

You immediately shed that protective wear and it seems ridiculous that you *ever* walked around in rain clothes just *expecting* it to rain!

Got it?

Ok, back to rage fire.

So, I can tell that despite my terseness and tight throat she is going to make me push through my feelings and deal with what I am *really* angry at.

But I did *not* expect what actually happened.

After pressing me to take some time to think about what I thought "the Universe" *was*, so I could more clearly examine where I was putting my anger she asked if we could do a short grounding meditation exercise.

I said yes because I knew it wouldn't make things *worse* but I was in a crappy head space so I wasn't particularly enthusiastic.

So the meditation begins and, having practiced lucid dreaming for over a decade, I'm pretty good at getting into the right space quickly.
As she's talking I see myself again, in my mind...

Only this time, that bat is gone and has been replaced by a sword. And this sword is particularly light. I've got my hand in my pocket and I'm struttin' and whistling and twirling that sword like Charlie Chaplin does his cane. My conscious mind decides that "no! I liked the *rage*! I need the *rage*!" and I try so hard to picture myself with that bat and that fire.

But I *can't*.

That image is just *dead*.

But the funny contrast between my two selves was this:

Rage Jess was holding the bat, looking for something to hit.

Sword Jess **knew** there was **nothing to hit**. There was no real threat. Nothing is *against* me.

As the meditation ended I was light as air and genuinely could do little other than laugh.

Everything was so clear and so obvious.

It was no wonder my darkest day was on the Winter Solstice. The longest night and ancient symbol of death and shedding. I shouted it in my previous post before I even realized what I'd said.

The married Jessica is dead!
The old me is dead – the me that would have just laid down and given up, that needed someone or something to blame.

And, coincidentally, an acquaintance asked if she could do a Goddess Card reading a few weeks ago,

Okay, I do not know what this means but it seemed fun...like something we'd do at a slumber party in 10th grade because we watched The Craft and wanted to be all ethereal.

This woman doesn't really know me and doesn't read my blog so she knows little about me.

The reading was encouraging. She said a lot of things that I needed to hear (kinda like when Neo visited the Oracle in The Matrix and HE said "I'm not the one" and she said "maybe next lifetime" and then he died but Trinity brought him back and then he realized Yes I AM the one so really she just said what needed to be said to put the right things in motion!) but she said one particular thing that really, really stuck.

She said:

"You've done a lot of intellectual and spiritual growth in the last few years but it feels burdensome to you. You don't know what to do with it. You seem to think it's creating conflict between yourself and others and you use your intellect and spirituality to separate yourself from the world. It's just this heavy thing you carry around but you don't realize that it is a tool, like a sword. You can be decisive and sharp. One day, you'll decide to pick it up."

I said, "Yeah like Alice slaying the jabberwocky."

And she said, "Yes but there is no jabberwocky."

Neo like a muhfuggah!

I get it. I get it deep, deep down. I've got a sword but I am *not* at war. The Universe is not *against* me, no need to shake my fist at it. That rant I went on last week? That was just my "Lieutenant Dan" moment. Now, I'm as calm as a cow.

My stepmom left me with another truth:

"Keep the goal steady, but be like water toward the path. When water meets a stone in the river, it flows around it and keeps moving."

Yes, my whole family is deep like that.

Going to college is my only goal. I am really unwilling to entertain anything else right now. I have no plan B. My focus is eagle-sharp.

So maybe that particular school was not the way. Maybe it's the right school and the wrong *time*. Who knows?

But what I do know is that rage is not the way.

Guilt

So, my youngest child is exhausting.
It feels like I cannot possibly make her happy. Nothing is enough. If we go swimming and get a treat she's mad that we didn't have time to go to the park, too.
The other kids get short with her for being ungrateful but I thought back to the situation with Jack and wondered if *this* was my fault...again.
I noticed that, with her more than my other kids, if she's upset I try to placate her quickly. I don't like when she was upset. I give in and resent her for being so powerful.
The only other person who made me feel that way was her father.
Uh oh...
Here we go again.
I don't want to *create* an entitled person who is incapable of being satisfied.
The older two aren't like this so what is different with *her*? Why are my boundaries so flexible with *just* her?
When I swear that she can't have ice cream, I bend a few hours later.
But why only with this child?
I realized that, subconsciously, I was guilt parenting.
The two older kids had a better recollection of what it was like when my ex and I were together. Jaya still says that "lasagna tastes like resentment" because of all the passive aggression that would be in the air at family gatherings when we lived in Tampa. She still won't eat it. Or chili for the same reason.

But Jordis was so young when we split she doesn't *remember* any discomfort. And that makes me feel like I *took* something from her. And treat her as such.

When Jaya was her age she was doing laundry, unloading dishes, keeping her hair brushed on her own, bathing regularly without me asking, doing her homework, reading for pleasure.

Jordis is not doing any of these things.

And why *should* she? The older ones do it for her.

Yeah, this isn't working.

But you know me, once I identify the problem I stop it immediately.

I gathered the kids and made a declaration that from now until I change my mind, *Jordis* is the oldest child.

This, of course, delighted her because she thought it meant she'd get some perks of some sort. Jaya, the oldest, usually gets to keep her electronics at night because she's responsible. Jordis's eyes gleamed.

She didn't realize it meant that I would expect from her all the things I had expected from Jaya. Jordis was now the go-to for chores and tasks. I expected her to resist and throw tantrums.

I got the complete opposite. She loved it. She absolutely loved it. She went above and beyond. She wiped windows I never asked her to wipe. She poured us drinks. She tried to make me coffee in the morning.

It was like liquid cocaine. But I drank it because I could see how proud she was of herself.

Jordis was bratty and high-maintenance because she didn't feel *needed*.

Jaya had a role because she is the oldest. She is the doer.

Jack had a role because he's "the man of the house." He's the guy who catches the lizards and shoo's the spiders.

Jordis was the baby.

That was it.

No wonder she was angry. I didn't give her a reason to feel *capable* or proud of herself.

Plus, just like the situation with Jack, when I caved to her whining and her fits I was *also* telling her she didn't have the tools to handle her feelings.

When I gave her the ice cream, yes, on one level it was just ice cream. On another it was, "the other two can handle disappointment, but you obviously can't, so here!"

Every time I relented, she got what she wanted but she *also* got her mother giving up on her and giving in. That's no message to send.

So the birth order flip-flop was designed to remedy all of that. I had to train myself to see her as capable. She had to *discover* that she was capable.

And the birth order flip-flop worked well for Jaya, too, who'd grown tired of being the go-to helper. She was always so irritated when she cooked something and the two littles asked for some, too. After a few weeks off she was sort of offended that no one asked her to cook anymore!

I also made a chart for the two little ones who were falling behind in their self-care after receiving tablets from my sister for Christmas.

I made them a deal. I wrote out that they were to nurture their bodies, minds and space every day.

This meant clean bodies, schoolwork done and space tidied.

For every five days in a row they got this done, they got their tablets back. If they missed a day, the five days started over. And *both* of them had get it done, so this helped them learn how to motivate each other. Any rude language used toward each other meant offender had to write five things they love about the other and a written apology, and the five things had to be new each time.

There have been some sweet letters and they've all grown super close. I always catch them hugging each other. I don't know if that's normal because I didn't grow up with siblings but I think it's precious.

In short, my parenting game is on point.

Single – February 2014

It's the day before Valentine's Day and it's been three years and four days since my divorce was finalized and there are twelve days until my 32nd birthday.

My blog is exactly three years old.

I am here to report that my stay-single-for-as-long-as-possible plan worked.

When I started this journey, my "self" had no outline. I was, as Liz Gilbert coined, a "permeable membrane." I had no boundaries. Everything and everyone came in and occupied me and seeped out as easily.

Now my outline is permanent marker thick-dark and solid.

Every week it seems I learn a new skill, and not arbitrary ones like "learning to play poker" but universal ones like "learning when to remove people from my life" and "learning to protect my space" like my inner Warrior leads me to do.

I have become katana-sharp at identifying and removing users and takers.

The sort of thick, heavy obligation and guilt that used to accompany my fear of people's reactions to my boundaries is gone.

I know there is a lot of romantic notion around the idea of fighting for someone. Rom-Coms and chick-flicks abound with people "fighting" for love and "fighting" for friendship.

I have found, in my life, that this has never been necessary.

And the relationships in which I'm always fighting to keep or please or satisfy or soothe someone, and vice versa, are the least healthy.

The people I can rely on the most in my day-to-day are actually really easy to get along with.

It's just easy. We're all fine and living our lives.

The friendships are as automatic and unconscious as breathing.

And that's become the driving force in my boundary making. I know it won't always be roses and cupcakes in all my relationships all the time, but I expect it to be pretty low-maintenance, easy - breezy at least the majority of the time.

I know I sound like a monster when I say, "I won't fight to keep you."

But I really exist in a space where I am comfortable with the ebbs and flows of human interaction. People come and go. People change. People are good for you when you're twenty-five and are neutral for you when you're thirty. People who you barely noticed when you were fifteen may be your rock when you are forty.

The *only* constant is change so the idea that your humans will always be exactly the same how-you-need-them-where-you-left-them is just silly.

And speaking of relationships...

Deep Sigh

Three years out of my divorce and I still haven't seriously dated. This seems to be more upsetting to the people around me than to myself so I'll take a moment to explain and respond to some of the well-meaning rhetoric that comes my way.

I've noticed that being uninterested in dating is what I imagine it's like to be a married couple uninterested in having children. People say to me, "don't worry, it'll happen..." as if I'm spending all my free time worried about the next time I make a poor choice in life partner.

It's an assumptive little microagression, implying I am are somehow incomplete without romantic cohabitation and coupling.

People also say "you'll find someone, you deserve to be happy."

Hmm, so apparently it's impossible to be happy alone. I guess I'm a walking and talking figment of my own imagination, then.

People say "you just need to find someone to sleep with, to get your groove back."

Uhhhh, anyone who knows me well knows I had a very thorough sexual exploration period. I have no doubt that my groove is just fine. Secondly, "just finding someone to sleep with" sounds like the least interesting thing ever to me right now. I spent a decade having sex with someone I neither respected nor loved. I think detached sex is the *last* thing I need.

Let me tell you a little something...

This period in my life is, by far, the happiest I have ever been. I got a katana in one hand and a black permanent marker in the other. I have eagle-sharp super focus on exactly what I want to do with my life. I am actually, for real, kinda in love with myself. I love the results of my parenting. I love my amazing group of friends. I love my relationship with my parents and grandparent and siblings.

I just feel really full, and solid, and clear, and sharp, and powerful right now.

I'm not sure if I would have gotten to this place had I not endured loneliness for a little while. I didn't run from my demons. I wasn't driven by insecurity to hurry up and couple up. I set a damn table for my Issues, served 'em tea and got well-acquainted until the demons and Issues weren't the scaries banging at the door or the creepies that came out in dark times.

I knew them by name.

"Alone" just doesn't scare me anymore. Not now and not even when I look into the distant future. The way I feel toward romance is the way I feel toward a pair of pink Converse. I'd really like to have it but I'm not exactly looking, and if I never get it I won't care *that* much. This finally feels more like a truth than a defense mechanism. But the ultimate reality about dating right now is this:

I absolutely have no room to nurture and water new relationships while I'm not even able to support me and mine independently. And to be frank, I don't feel I've *earned* that room. And that's okay. *I* am comfortable with that.

I have plenty of "me time."
I have plenty of relationships that nourish me.
I'd love to spend time with new people but, if it isn't easy and low-maintenance, then later for

it.

A new romantic relationship is a time-suck. It requires a lot of resources.

I don't have those things right now.

That said, of course I know that, despite my Spock-like love of rationality and cost/benefit calculations, sometimes life is just random. I am *open* to the idea of a relationship. But (Inner Spock won't relent) given my lack of availability, I don't see it happening.

Right now I'm the ringleader of a traveling circus. If a man sees my dazzling, spectacular show and can run real fast and hop on the train I'd be happy to accommodate him as long as he's willing to do some work. But the show must go on, and this train doesn't make special stops…

Tomorrow I am going to a friend's house. Fellow single parents and our kids will get together to celebrate our singleness. Only this time, it's not irony. I'm not jealous of my friends in relationships. I really celebrate my singleness. Jessica Vivian 2.0 is here and I'm wild and fierce and brave and clear and sharp and dangerous and slippery and unstoppable.

All by my big girl self.

The End

Afterword

Hey there, friend.
So, I bet you're wondering how things turned out.

Well, I'm still single though I have been on a few dates. It's still not a priority to me right now but I have certainly softened to the idea.

I did make it back into college! Yay!!!
I was only able to pay for two classes but those two classes are going well. Once my GPA is up I'll be able to apply for Financial Aid and go full steam.
One amazing thing happened, though!
I settled on a TESOL program (this is so I can teach English abroad) and couldn't afford it. I'd helped a lot of single moms over the last few years and decided to just go out on a limb and see if anyone would help me. I made a fundraiser site and shared it on Facebook. Then, later that morning I was playing with a friend's deck of Tarot cards and picked the Wheel of Fortune.
When I checked my fundraiser site that evening I'd raised the 2K I needed to get my TESOL program started.
How d'ya like dem apples?

As for my blog, I closed it shortly after that last chapter. I just got tired of talking about myself, frankly. I was tired of my own voice. I had nothing to say. The blog was about sharing my feelings and started to be about feeding my ego. I felt like I was regressing. Everything is moving forward and I'm trying to be less cerebral and more action-oriented. So it had to go.

Looking back over those years I am most taken by the amount of spontaneous love being exchanged. People, without any logical reason, just sharing and giving in love. Single-parents wrote me and said "I wish I had a community like yours in my town!" and I'd always respond with "So make one!"

"How?" they always asked and really I had no answer. I'd suggest just asking their friends over to get real but not until now did I truly understand what makes it happen.

Vulnerability.

By putting my junk out there so freely, I made myself vulnerable.

Being vulnerable is a lot like being the first one on the dance floor at prom – which I was, with my friend Elizabeth, off to the side a bit where no one would *really* notice but visible *enough*.

If the *goal* of the evening is having a good time, *someone* has to get the party started.

It feels really icky and alone and awkward. Everyone is just looking at you.

I knew we looked like the weird girls. I mean, we *were* weird girls. That's a whole other book...

But eventually someone joined in. And someone else. And someone else.

Before you know it, it's a sho nuff party. No one remembers or cares who got on the dance floor first, or how awkward they were, or whether or not they could dance. They are just relieved they didn't have to go first and grateful the fun is happening before it's too late and we all have to go home.

Connecting is kind of like that.

I wanted to *connect* and help people. I wanted support.

So I put my junk out there *first*. And other people joined me. And someone else. And someone else until communities were built and connections were made.

I'm sure people were relieved and grateful for the communities, even if they were temporary.

Now is the time for me to say thanks to all my peeps.

I'd like to thank all my volunteer editors: Simon, Toyia, Carrieann, Rachel, Aimee and Michelle.   I'd like to thank Chris for being a really stellar best friend and for the picture of the pancakes because you know I'm not making any.

I'd like to thank the Wolfpack, current and former and all over the place, for just being the most powerful, electric, gentle, complex, multifaceted bunch of broads I've ever encountered.

I'd like to thank the Sistas Without Mistas across the globe. We got dis.

I'd like to thank My MOM!!! You have NEVER EVER EVER EVER let me fall on my face. You have always believed in me, even when I don't and even when maybe I don't deserve it, ha!

I'd like to thank my sister. You're the brains of this operation. How we haven't driven you mad is beyond me.

I'd like to thank a certain blog reader who donated the money to help me apply to more colleges. Just....thank you so much for believing in me.

I'd like to thank Papa, Vicky and Amanda for being cool.

I'd like to thank My Dad and Stepmom, Carly for all the pep talks and listening ears.

I'd like to thank my ex-husband most of all. I don't know why we crossed paths. Perhaps it was only to facilitate the inclusion of those three little souls on this Earth. But thank you for that. And I hope, from the deepest depths of my soul, you get what you need so that you can have peace and believe in yourself. Despite everything, I root for you.

And I'd like to thank my amazing babies. Jaya the Wise, Jack the Gentle, Jordis The Snuggly.

I love you all to the moon and back.

J.Viv